Consumer and Family
Science Depart.
Purdue University Extension Svc
Marion County
9245 N. Meridian Street, #118
Indianapolis, IN 46260-1312
(317)848-7351 or 253-0871 ext. 123

# Cornucopia

## THE LORE OF
## FRUITS & VEGETABLES

## ANNIE LISE ROBERTS

KNICKERBOCKER
PRESS

Published by
Knickerbocker Press
276 Fifth Avenue
New York, NY 10001

Produced by Saraband Inc., PO Box 0032,
Rowayton, Connecticut 06853

Copyright © 1998 Saraband Inc.

Design © Ziga Design

ISBN 1-57715-036-8

Printed in China

10  9  8  7  6  5  4  3  2  1

***Above:*** Summer, *by Giuseppe Arcimboldo
(1527–1593).*
***Page 4:*** Earth, *from the series*
The Elements, *by Jan Breughel (1568–1625).*

**Note:** The recipes on pages 39 and 79 include the use of raw eggs,
which may contain harmful bacteria. The reader should take
note that these carry the risk of inducing sickness and should
not be served to minors, the elderly, or any person whose immune
system is compromised. Dietary restrictions should be considered before consuming alcohol and other ingredients in the
recipes in this book. Always use fresh ingredients and exercise
extreme caution in the storage of foods. No responsibility can
be taken by the publisher for adverse reactions to these recipes
or inadequate storage precautions after their preparation.

FOR MY ZIGA BOYZ,

*Chuck — without whose infinite patience
I could not operate in this world*

*Michael and David — who are growing up*
VELOCIUS QUAM ASPARAGI COQUANTUR

# CONTENTS

# INTRODUCTION

SINCE THE BEGINNING OF HUMAN HISTORY, plants have been our primary food source, without which life could not be sustained. It is no wonder, therefore, that the history of agriculture reveals so much about civilization itself. Individual plants are the sacred and profane roots of entire cultures—corn for the Incas and olives for the Greeks. Meanwhile, new varieties and imports are the surprise and delight of creative cuisines.

The ancient Greek and Roman agriculturalists were interested in fruits, vegetables, grains, and nuts and made extensive improvements in their cultivation. The Greeks, for example, originated the technique of grafting (which is still used today), while the Romans developed no fewer than twenty-five varieties of apples and thirty-eight of pears. Pliny the Elder (d. AD 79) traveled widely to write *Historia Naturalis*, a thirty-seven–volume encyclopedia of natural history, which contains information on many fruits and vegetables, along with recommendations on the use of some and stern warnings against the uses of others. The Roman gastronome Apicuis wrote the first known cookbook in AD 14 and influenced most Western cuisines as a result.

While Arab travelers introduced new foods to Europe from the East, conquering Romans spread new plants and techniques of cultivation throughout the Empire. During the Dark Ages, many foods disappeared, and both culinary and medicinal skills were lost until their reintroduction during the Renaissance.

Europe's demand for spices fostered the growth of the world's most powerful navies in Italy, Portugal, Spain, Holland, and England; the most celebrated explorers, including Christopher Columbus, were seeking alternative spice routes to the famed "Indies." They failed to find a new source for peppercorn, but instead returned with corn, squash, beans, tomatoes, potatoes, avocados, and pineapples. In turn, the colonizers introduced many Old World foods to the Americas, including pears, apples, peaches, carrots, chickpeas, bananas, figs, and citrus fruits. The Spanish missionaries were outstanding agronomists who helped establish the fertile California Valley as an agricultural center by adapting introduced fruits and vegetables.

From the Mediterranean basin, comestibles were transported eastward by sea and, more gradually, by land, to northern Europe. In 1533 Catherine de Médici left Florence to marry Henri II of France. There she not only reigned over her subjects, but became queen of haute cuisine. Her Italian chefs acquainted France with artichokes, spinach, broccoli, and South American beans, among other foods. Not all were accepted in northern Europe as edibles, but many of these new plants were prized for their medicinal applications. The English herbalist and physician John Gerard, among others, documented the newly discovered plants, intending to inform—albeit frequently misinforming—people on their uses.

Cuisines expanded and the culinary arts flourished during the 17th and 18th centuries. Exotic fruits and vegetables were prized by the elite, who competed in being the first to dine on, as well as to grow, the new foods. Artichokes, carrots, melons, oranges, pineapples, and pomegranates all enjoyed the limelight at one time or another as the darlings of the privileged. Louis XIV's legendary orchard and his

master gardener, Jean-Baptiste de la Quintinie, awed the Continent with such tropical plants as oranges and pineapple.

During the Industrial Revolution great strides were made in food transportation for the mass market, initially via rail and later by road, while advances were also made in techniques for preserving food. Until recently, foods were seasonal, and the anticipation of spring and its bounty was inspirational. Sweet peas and cherries were closely associated with spring; autumn was welcomed by apple pies and pumpkins. Through long winters, Hubbard squashes, dried fruits, and many delicious preserved and pickled foods brought comfort and nourishment. Today, almost all fruits and vegetables are available year-round—but with convenience comes sacrifice in lack of flavor and texture and excessive use of pesticides. Nostalgia for better-quality produce is stimulating the growth of local farmers' markets and organic gardens.

The horn of the cornucopia, overflowing with fruits and flowers, is the quintessential symbol of abundance. In Greek mythology, the horn was filled with an inexhaustible supply of whatever the possessor wished. This book explores individual fruits and vegetables, prominent in Western culture, through legend, lore, art, poetry, and literary observations. Although technically olives, eggplants (aubergines), cucumbers, peas, avocados, corn, tomatoes, potatoes, peppers, and squash are fruits, this book divides fruits and vegetables according to their culinary uses: savory plants are presented with vegetables and the sweet ones are considered fruits. The mission of this book is to delight the reader with a wealth of interesting lore about the plants being prepared in kitchens across the Western world. 🌱 🌱 🌱 🌱

FRUITS

FRUIT, THE ORIGINAL DESSERT, HAS ALWAYS appealed to our innate craving for sweets. Unlike many foods, fruits require no preparation: most can be eaten directly from the harvesting hand. They are a symbol of fertility, life, and abundance, representing nature's bounty.

*Frui*, Latin for fruit, means to enjoy. These are the foods of celebration, featuring prominently in ancient mythology and religious rites.

While most fruits have a negligible amount of vitamins (with the exception of vitamins A and C), compared to dairy products or meat, fruits have sugars that are easily assimilated, and fresh fruit provides essential organic acids.

The most sensuous of foods, fruits have been prized since time immemorial, each for its own distinct flavor, sweetness, shape, texture, and color. Luscious fruits are the archetypal aphrodisiac, associated with seduction and temptation since the first couple, Adam and Eve, ate the forbidden fruit. 🍇 🍇 🍇 🍇 🍇

*Jews and Christians are convinced that Adam and Eve wore out their welcome in the Garden of Eden when they ate the apple. Polynesian Islanders are quite sure that it was a banana they ate; descendants of the Carib Indians are firm in their belief that it was a papaya; and Trobriand Islanders are certain that it was a pineapple. Since the beginning of time, men and women have always been in trouble because of one fruit or another.*

— MARGARET MEAD
*American anthropologist*

**Opposite**: *A still life of melon, grapes, cherries and strawberries by Severin Roesen, mid-1800s.*

# PEACH

*Prunus persica*

The ancient history of the peach began in China, where it still grows wild. There, peaches are weighted with significance, symbolizing long life and immortality. Since the Ch'in dynasty (2nd century BC), the Chinese have placed bowls of peaches in tombs to preserve bodies from deterioration. A recently discovered tomb dating from this era contained a mummy and a bowl of peaches, both of which were remarkably well-preserved.

Throughout the centuries in China, birthdays have been celebrated with a peach-shaped steamed roll called *shoutao*, which means "long life peach," while a treasured birthday gift might be a porcelain object decorated with peach blossoms. The peach is a symbol of longevity because in the Chinese conception of the garden of paradise, the peach tree bears fruit only once every 3,000 years. New Year festivities include a gift of blossoms for good luck and peaches eaten for long life. Because the words marriage and peach share

## SIDELIGHTS

*When the peach arrived in Persia from China, it flourished so well that the fruit was mistakenly thought to have originated there. It was thus called "Persian Apple" by Pliny, the Roman naturalist, and given the botanical name* PRUNUS PERSICA.

*The peach has a low sugar content and is high in vitamins A and C and mineral salts.*

*The nectarine,* PRUNUS PERSICA *var.* NECTARINA, *is not a cross between a plum and a peach, as is frequently believed, but a fuzzless peach. It was named after nectar, the drink of the classical gods.*

the same Chinese character, the two are often associated in China.

In Christian art, a peach with a leaf signifies the unity of truth and silence.

> *Training is everything.*
> *The peach was once a bitter almond.*
> —MARK TWAIN, *Pudd'n head Wilson* (1894)

In the West, the peach is associated with sensuality because of its delicate flower, voluptuous shape, velvety skin, and creamy pink fleshy color. Renoir had his students paint still lifes of peaches to better understand the skin tones of women's breasts. William Fahey wrote about the peach, "All pink and yellow and dimpled and juicily cleft as Renoir's *baigneuses* [bathers]."

Beyond symbolism, the peach also has potent culinary powers. When Madame Récamier, Paris's most celebrated hostess of the 19th century, fell sick and refused food, it was said that her life was saved by peaches in syrup and cream. Their delicacy restored her appetite and her will to live.

Peaches and cream are natural companions, and there is no dearth of recipes for the combination. Southern Europeans slice a freshly picked peach directly into a glass of local wine to savor at the end of the meal. Although often eaten for dessert, the peach's acidity makes it very good in savory dishes as well. Peach kernels, inside the pit, add flavor to syrups and are made into a brandy the French call *noyau*.

Introduced to the New World by Spanish explorers, peaches grew well in American soil. Many Native Americans fully appreciated the luscious fruit, and the Natchez tribe named one of their months for it. Cultivation of peach trees spread so quickly among tribes that in 1663 William Penn wrote, "not an Indian plantation is without them."

## SIDELIGHTS

*Peach trees require at least two months of cool, dormant winter weather to rejuvenate and produce fruit again in the spring.*

*Peaches are categorized as either clingstones or freestones, depending on how easily the flesh pulls away from the pit.*

***Opposite, below:*** *Ripe peaches conjure images of shortcake, cobbler, and other delights of summer.*

***Above:*** *Renoir's series of bathers showed the delicate, peach-colored flesh tones for which the Impressionist master is famous.*

# CHERRY
### *Prunus avium, Prunus cerasus*

The cherry is one of the few crops that is still truly seasonal, with a preciously short season. Cherries are divided into sweet and tart varieties. Sweet cherries *(P. avium),* are mainly eaten fresh and range in color from yellow to nearly black. Unlike most fruit, the size of sweet cherries does affect their flavor—larger fruits taste better and have a finer texture.

Tart cherries *(P. cerasus)* range in color from light to dark red and grow on small trees. Primarily, these types are canned, frozen, made into brandy, and used in savory dishes. Germans and Scandinavians use the sour cherry in venison and pork recipes. Other popular dishes that use tart cherries are Hungarian sour cherry soup and French Montmorency duckling.

Liqueurs made from cherries include Heering, a cherry brandy from Denmark, and Kirsch, made in the Alsace region, on the German/French border. Kirsch is made from the entire cherry; the crushed pit accounts for the slight almond flavor. Maraschino, a liqueur made from the Marasca cherry, originates from the Dalmatian coast of the Balkans.

The Assyrians and Babylonians who first cultivated the cherry called it *karsu,* which evolved into the Latin *cerasus,* and eventually into the old French word *cherise* (*cerise* in contemporary French), and the English word cherry.

The delicate fruit requires specific growing conditions, limiting the areas where it can be grown. Leaders in production

*Cherry-ripe, ripe, ripe, I cry,*
*Full and fair ones; come and buy:*
*If so be, you ask me where*
*They do grow? I answer, There,*
*Where Julia's lips do smile;*
*There's the land, or cherry-isle,*
*Whose plantations fully show*
*All the year where cherries grow.*

— ROBERT HERRICK

*17th-century English poet*

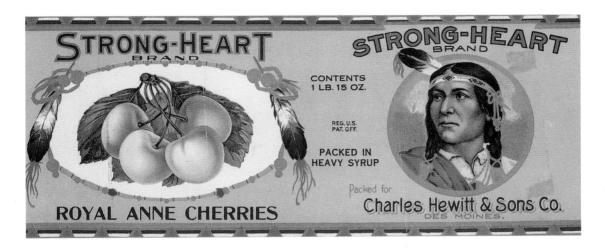

include the United States, parts of the former Soviet Union, Italy, France, and Germany. The United States is the biggest producer, with ideal conditions in the Pacific Northwest for sweet cherries and around Lake Michigan for tart cherries.

## It is no use making two bites of a cherry.

—PROVERB

New York City's Broadway jogs west at East 10th Street because of a cherry tree that once stood there. Under this cherry tree, innkeeper Hendrick Brevoort smoked his pipe on warm evenings. When he learned that the extension of Broadway involved cutting down his favorite tree, he convinced city officials that New York would never grow as far as his tavern. Broadway was diverted to save the cherry tree.

## SIDELIGHTS

*In Japan, a variety of cherry tree is grown exclusively for its exquisite blossoms.*

*In 1912, the mayor of Tokyo gave the city of Washington, D.C., the cherry trees that surround the Tidal Basin.*

*Bing cherries, favored for eating, are a variety developed by Seth Lewelling in 1875. The Oregon grower named the cherry for one of the Chinese workers in his orchard.*

**Above:** *An old-fashioned label for sweet cherries, featuring a Native American trademark in the romantic style of the early 20th century.*

**Left:** *Always a welcome sight— the first cherries of the season.*

# ¶LUM

*Prunus family*

The food authority Waverly Root cites the plum as "one of the world's most luscious fruits." He is not alone in his high opinion of this fruit, as the word plum itself means something excellent or desirable.

Plums originate from Europe, North America, and Asia. The European plum was probably developed by the ancient Romans, who were diligent in cultivating and improving the wild plum. Pliny the Elder, the Roman naturalist, wrote, "no other tree has been so ingeniously crossed."

*"Life's a pudding full of plums…"*

—GILBERT & SULLIVAN

*The Gondoliers (1889)*

## S I D E L I G H T S

*The French plum variety Reine Claude was named after Queen Claude, wife of Francis I. The honor was dubious, however, as it is said the plum's deep cleft was reminiscent of her enormous royal backside.*

*The plum was introduced to England in 1725 by Sir Thomas Gage and was called the Greengage (a name now reserved for a small yellow-green variety).*

*Thomas Culpeper, the 18th-century English herbalist, recommended the plum "both in health and sickness, to relish the mouth and stomach…." To cure ringworm, he prescribed a mixture of plum leaves boiled in vinegar.*

*Plums can be divided into the freestones and clingstones. The best-known freestone is the Italian prune plum.*

*In Europe the small, sweet Mirabella is cherished for its perfume.*

I have eaten
the plums
that were in
the icebox
and which
you were probably
saving
for breakfast
Forgive me
they were delicious

—WILLIAM CARLOS WILLIAMS
*20th-century American poet*

Today, the countless varieties are a result of crossing three species, the European plum (*P. domestica*), American plum (*P. americana*), and Japanese plum (*P. salicina*). The plum has the greatest number of species and varieties in the *Prunus* genus, which includes the apricot, peach, cherry, and almond. The different species of plums range from small olive-sized fruits to over three inches in diameter, and their color can vary from a light yellow to a deep, near-black, purple.

The New World plum, a wild fruit growing all over the Americas, was a favorite of many tribes and was served at the first Thanksgiving supper in 1621. But it was tougher and more tart than those the early colonists had eaten in Europe. They missed the sweet, plump European plum (which had the benefit of 2,000 years of cultivation) and planted orchards from imported seeds.

The Japanese plum is actually a native of China, but was adopted, cultivated, and improved upon by the Japanese. Introduced to the United States in 1870, it is now second in production only to the European plum.

Plums are eaten fresh, dried, or made into preserves, jams, and sweet pickles. In the Balkans, a dry, slightly bitter brandy called slivovitz is made. The oldest plum is the sloe, a small bitter fruit used to make sloe gin. The English make a "cheese" or fruit butter from the Damson plum. In France, the d'Agen plum is grown in the same region as Armagnac, and in the regional cuisine, the fruit often accompanies the brandy.

*Opposite:* (top) *An elegant drawing from the 19th-century* British *Gardener's Assistant.* **Above:** *A contemporary photograph of ripe Friar plums on the tree.*

## RECIPE

**Brandied Plum Sauce**
1 pound ripe plums, pitted and chopped
¼ cup sugar
¼ cup brandy
Lemon zest

In a saucepan, place all ingredients and bring to a boil. Cover and simmer until the plums soften. Stir often.

Purée the mixture and then pass the sauce through a fine sieve, pressing all the juice through.

Add more sugar to taste. If the sauce is too thick, add water or more brandy.

Use warmed-up over ice cream or cake.

# APRICOT
## *Prunus armeniaca*

The apricot features a glowing velvety skin, while its flesh is imbued with tangy flavor. A longtime favorite of patisserie chefs, apricot glazes and jams impart a special touch to many desserts.

Eastern countries call the apricot "moon of the faithful," and the ancient Persians called them "sun eggs." In Greek mythology, the Golden Apples of the Hesperides were, in fact, apricots. The Romans called them *praecocium,* meaning precocious, since they ripen in early summer well in advance of plums and peaches. The English name comes from the Latin *praecox.*

## SIDELIGHTS

*The apricot is an excellent source of carotene (vitamin A), which helps fight infection and prevents night blindness. It is also rich in potassium and fiber.*

*Allusions to the apricot's alleged aphrodisiac qualities appear in Shakespeare's A MIDSUMMER NIGHT'S DREAM, when the Queen of Fairies lures her lover with the luscious, tangy fruit.*

> *The Armenian plum, imported from foreign parts, is the only plum which recommends itself even by its scent.*
>
> — PLINY THE ELDER, *1st century AD*

Because the trees bloom early, apricots are susceptible to frost. The fruit is so delicate that it does not travel well—even via climatized transportation—so fully ripened apricots are not readily available outside of the areas where they are grown. However, the apricot dries very well, retaining all its original flavor and nutritional qualities.

The fruit is a drupe, or a freestone fruit, meaning that it is fleshy and one-seeded—as are plums, cherries, almonds, and peaches. Originally from ancient China and cultivated since 2,000 BC, the apricot came

to flourish throughout the Far and Middle East, where the fruit has been sun dried for thousands of years. Although introduced to Italy via Armenia (hence the Latin name *Prunus armeniaca*), the apricot was not widely known in Europe until the 15th century.

The apricot was introduced to the United States by the Spanish and reached the fertile valleys of California in the early 18th century via the Franciscan founders of the mission. Today, California is the world's largest producer. Other producers include Syria, Chile, Iran, Australia, and South Africa.

### SIDELIGHTS

*In the Middle East, dried apricot "leather" and apricot wines are widely available.*

*The pit protects a small kernel that resembles an almond and is used in marzipan, amaretto, preserves, and brandies.*

---

## The apricot is shining in a sweet brightness of golden velvet.

— JOHN RUSKIN, *19th-century British social reformer and art critic*

---

*Below: The famous Moor Park apricot, as painted for* The Practical Gardener *in 1871.*

### RECIPE

**Apricot Preserves**
1½ cups dried apricot halves, coarsely puréed in a food processor
2 cups water
¾ cup sugar
Juice of one lemon
½ tsp. almond extract
2 tbs. brandy

Cook all ingredients in heavy saucepan over medium heat for 30 minutes or until thick. Stir occasionally.

Cool and refrigerate in airtight container. It will store for several months. Use as a glaze for tarts or ham, cookie filling, warmed up as a sauce for cake or ice cream and, of course, as a spread for breads.

**SIDELIGHTS**

*Pears are a good source of fiber, potassium, and vitamins A, B, and C.*

*They are believed to promote healthier hair and a clear complexion.*

*The Comice, nicknamed the "queen of pears," is considered by many to have the finest flavor and texture.*

# $\mathcal{P}$EAR

*Pyrus communis*

*A pear should have such a texture as leads to silent consumption.*

— EDWARD BUNYARD, *20th-century English author*

Because wild pears are bitter and gritty, cultivation of the fruit has been essential. As Alexander Dumas wrote in the *Grand Dictionaries de Cuisine:*

"*The pear which comes from cultivated stock is one of our best fruits.… If we compare the small size, hardness and bitter taste of the wild pear with the huge size, sweetness and softness of many of our beautiful fruits, we realize what a marvelous influence cultivation has had.*"

Pears are best when picked before fully ripening. If left on the tree, the hard cells in the flesh, called grit, become more pronounced. The fruit is delicate and best eaten immediately before it becomes too ripe. The saying "One must stay up at night to eat a pear, watching and waiting," indicates the elusiveness of the perfect moment for enjoying a pear.

## The gift of the gods.

— HOMER

The pear dates back thousands of years and is thought to have originated in China, although it has been cultivated in Europe for centuries. Like the apple, each seed produces its own variety, and today there are over 5,000 cultivated varieties worldwide.

The fruit was spread throughout the North American St. Lawrence Valley by French Jesuit missionaries. They introduced pears to the Iroquois, who recognized their value and began to cultivate them. Pears were brought to the American West Coast by the Spanish missionary friars. Today the fruit is grown in temperate climates on five continents.

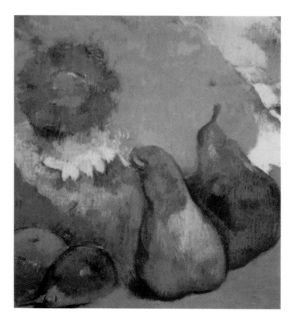

---

### RECIPE

**Poires Belle Hélène**
4 medium pears with long stems
4 cups water
1 cup sugar
Juice of one lemon
Lemon zests
Chocolate, melted in a double boiler.

In a saucepan, boil water, sugar, lemon juice and zests over low heat for 5 minutes. Peel and core from the bottom, leaving the pear whole. Poach pears in the sugar/water syrup until tender.

Thin the melted chocolate with the sugar/water syrup to desired consistency. Place cooled pears over a bed of vanilla ice cream. Drizzle melted chocolate sauce over them and garnish with lemon zests.

---

**Opposite, top:** *Pears form the centerpiece of an elegant Old World table setting.*

**Above:** *Fresh pears may be combined with other fruits to make a delicious compote.*

**Left:** *Detail from a Gauguin still life with pears.*

## SIDELIGHTS

*There are countless varieties of apples because each seed produces its own individual fruit. To propagate a consistent variety beyond the life of a particular tree, orchards must be the result of grafting root stock.*

*Of the more than 7,000 cultivated varieties of apples, most were developed in the 18th and 19th centuries. About 100 varieties are grown commercially.*

*The apple is the oldest cultivated fruit, having been grown since the beginning of the Stone Age.*

**Above:** *Engraving of an antique cider mill.*

**Opposite:** *Romance blooms in a Victorian-era orchard.*

# APPLE

*Malus pumila*

Throughout history, the apple has been the standard referent for other fruits and vegetables: lemons and peaches were called "Persian apples" when introduced to Europe; eggplants were known as "mad apples" and tomatoes as "love apples." The French word for potatoes, *pommes de terre,* means "apples of the earth"; dates were called "finger apples" and pomegranates "apples of Carthage"; while the Greeks referred to apricots as "Armenian apples."

Apples are native to Europe and West Asia; they were introduced to North America in the 17th century. For centuries, the basic apple product was cider. Vinegar was made from the cider and used for preserving and as a yeast for baking. Today, the majority of apples grown in Europe are still used for cider.

The ancient Greeks associated apples with women: apples symbolized breasts, the seeds, pregnancy, and an apple tree, a child-bearing woman. Sacred to the goddess of love, Aphrodite, apples have been integral to customs of courtship and marriage. The contemporary American tradition of showering rice or almonds on newlyweds evolved from the custom of throwing apples at weddings, and for centuries, there was a Greek custom of tossing apples at a loved one. Throughout classical mythology, where there is love, there is an apple.

---

*When I've prodded them, [people] have mumbled of apples: biting into them, feeling the cold juice flow into the mouth corners, hearing the snap of skin and pulp.*

— M.F.K. FISHER,
*20th-century American food and travel author*

---

The apple is, of course, legendary as the origin of humanity's downfall, when Eve ate the forbidden fruit from the Tree of Knowledge. But Eve's fruit is not actually specified in the Bible as an apple, and it may equally well have been a quince, a pomegranate, or a pear.

The ritual of bobbing for apples at Halloween began as a more serious love ritual in Ireland. On the eve of Samhain, the 31st of October, the official end of summer, young Celts tried to influence their marital fate by assigning names to each apple: the one they bit into represented their future spouse.

In America, at the turn of the century, determining one's future mate was done by naming apple seeds and then shooting them from between the fingers to the ceiling. The seed that reached the ceiling would be the purported spouse-to-be. This custom dates back almost 2,000

**SIDELIGHTS**

*Does an apple a day keep the doctor away? Well, yes, raw apples help the digestive juices kill germs in the stomach.*

*The apple's Latin name,* MALUS, *(evil), suggests its role in the downfall of man.*

years—the Latin author Horace wrote about the same ritual in 35 BC.

John Chapman, a.k.a. Johnny Appleseed, roamed the wild frontier of the American Ohio River Valley in the early 1800s. He carried a bag of apple seeds, which he traded, sold, or planted, and he is credited with establishing more than 10,000 square miles of orchards. He preached a Swedenborgian philosophy, was regarded as a healer, and befriended Native Americans and settlers alike, winning a place in folklore.

***Above:*** *Flemish apple pickers by Emile Claus in* Our Country *(1905).*

***Opposite, below:*** Adam and Eve, *in the famous painting by Lucas Cranach.*

**Legend**

In Greek legend, the swift-footed huntress Atalanta agreed to marry any suitor who could beat her in a foot race. Those who lost, however, would be speared to death. Many young men tried and failed, losing the race and their lives. One hopeful suitor, Hippomenes, appealed to the goddess Aphrodite for assistance. She presented him with three golden apples and instructed him to throw them down in the course of the race. Atalanta was so captivated by the beautiful fruit that she paused to pick up the apples, losing the race, and thus her celibacy, to Hippomenes.

*The apple is our national fruit. . . . The American sun paints himself in these glowing balls amid the green leaves. Man would be more solitary, less friended, less supported, if the land yielded only the useful maize and potato, and withheld this ornamental and social fruit.*

— RALPH WALDO EMERSON, *Journals*

### Foretelling Love

If you want to know the initial of your future mate's given name, peel an apple in one long strip and throw the peel over your left shoulder. The strip will form the initial of your sweetheart where it falls. Or, just before midnight on Halloween, take an apple and a candle into a dark room. Stand before a mirror and cut the apple into small pieces. Throw one piece over your right shoulder and eat the rest while combing your hair. Do not look behind you. At midnight, your true love's face will appear in the mirror.

### EXPRESSIONS

*Apple of my eye: someone or something much loved. The saying originally referred to the eye's pupil, which was believed to be spherical.*

*Apples and Pears: in Cockney rhyming slang, means "stairs."*

*The Big Apple: The origin of New York City's nickname is unknown. It may be associated with a 1930s dance called the "Big Apple."*

*As American as Apple Pie: refers to something quintessentially American.*

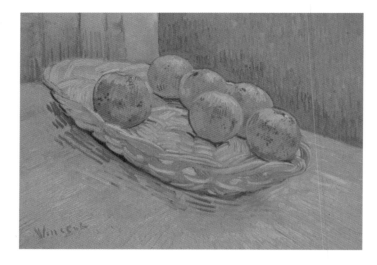

## SIDELIGHTS

*Early oranges were small and bitter, similar to Seville oranges.*

*The Medici family coat of arms includes five golden balls that are emblematic of oranges.*

*The tradition of brides wearing sprigs of the exquisite, pungent orange blossom refers back to classical mythology, in which Jupiter gave Juno a golden orange for their nuptials.*

*Although the kumquat, whose Cantonese name means "gold orange," has been around since the 17th century, it is still a rarity. The tiny orange is eaten whole— peel, seeds and all.*

***Opposite and above:*** *The orange's glowing colors have made it the subject of many works of art, including the still life above by Vincent Van Gogh, the William Morris tapestry at the top of the facing page, and the vibrant painting of an Egyptian fruit stall.*

# ORANGE

*Citrus sinensis*

Oranges came to symbolize opulence and luxury in France during the reign of Charles VIII, which gave rise to the cult of the orangery. Such a structure, devoted to the purpose of cultivating exotic plants in an inhospitable climate, showed the extravagance and means of its owner. The most famous orangery was built for Louis XIV at Versailles. It held 1,200 potted orange trees and required an army of gardeners, who rotated the trees and brought them outside on sunny days. Branches of orange blossoms graced the tables of the aristocracy, while the fragrant flowers lent their intoxicating scent to baths, and the aroma found its way into cuisine. These European oranges were largely decorative and rather small and bitter, but they were sometimes used for marmalade. Oranges intended for eating were imported either from Portugal or the East.

This ancient fruit originated in China, where it has been cultivated since 2,400 BC. Oranges traveled with Arab traders, being established along the way in India, North Africa, and

the Mediterranean. By the 11th century, oranges were widespread in both the south of France and Italy.

There are three main commercial varieties of oranges: the sweet orange, *C. sinensis*, which includes the Valencia and Navel orange; the Mandarin, *C. reticulata*, also called Clementine; and the sour orange, *C. aurantium*, which is known as the Seville orange and is used for marmalades, and for flavoring candies and liqueurs.

The English word orange is derived from the Dravidian Indian word *narayam*, which translates to "perfume within." The Spanish word for orange is *naranja*.

The orange tree blooms and bears fruit at the same time, offering a distinctly beautiful medley of deep green, white, and orange hues.

Oranges are picked when fully ripe, as the fruit does not ripen further once it is picked. An orange's color is not affected by ripeness, but rather by the temperature while the fruit is still on the tree. Oranges grown in the tropics remain green.

*California's a wonderful place to live—if you happen to be an orange.*

—FRED ALLEN
*American humorist (1989)*

**SIDELIGHTS**

*Musicians caution that if one sucks on a lemon within sight of a trumpeter, his lips will so pucker that he will be unable to play.*

*Limes contain more sugar and acid than lemons.*

*In Central America limes, more readily available than lemons, are used extensively in cuisine. Mexico produces the largest number of limes.*

*Limes are used by Malaysian sorcerers to send messages between lovers.*

*Lime is said to remove rust from clothing.*

# LEMON, LIME AND CITRON

## Citrus limon, Citrus aurantifolia, Citrus medica

Lemons and limes, often interchangeable, are similar for culinary purposes. The reason some cultures use one rather than the other is climactic: The lime tree prefers a tropical climate with moist air, while the lemon tree thrives in drier air and is more resistant to frost. Both are more climate-sensitive than the orange tree. Lemons and limes traveled the trade routes west from Asia, to North Africa, and to the other countries surrounding the Mediterranean Sea.

Although limes are available in sweet and sour varieties, Europeans and Americans generally use only sour limes. Beginning in the 1590s, they were used to pre-

*Knowst thou the land where the lemon trees bloom,*
*where the gold orange glows in the deep thicket's gloom.*
—JOHANN W. VON GOETHE
*Wilhelm Meister's Apprenticeship (1830)*

vent scurvy among British sailors, and by 1790 a concoction of lime and rum was a mandatory drink (the origin of the pejorative name "Limey" for British sailors). Although lemons—an equally good source of vitamin C—could have been used, limes were readily available from the British colony of Jamaica. Lemons, on the other hand, could only be imported from the Mediterranean countries, with whom the British were often at odds, if not at war.

Although the lemon is associated, in some cultures, with poor cars and bad merchandise, it is in fact a versatile and invaluable fruit. Essential oil from lemon zest is used in medicine, household products, and cosmetics. Lemon juice slows discoloring of cut fruits and vegetables, adds flavor to many foods, and is rich in pectin, used for making jams and jellies. Lemonade has refreshed countless palates all over the world for centuries.

The citron is the grandfather of both the lemon and the lime. It resembles a lemon but is larger and more coarse-skinned. It is used cooked, candied, or preserved and is not commonly found in Europe or the United States. In India, the citron flesh is pickled in a curried liquid, while in Israel the citron, called an *etrog,* is available for a very short, seven-day season after Yom Kippur. In France, a jellied paste made of citron is called *pate de cédrat.*

**Above:** *An 18th-century colored gravure from Italy depicts a lemon overhanging luxurious villas and gardens.*

**Left:** *A Sicilian citrus orchard provides a bountiful harvest in this 1911 painting by Alberto Pusa.*

**Opposite, below:** *Comparative sizes of the popular cousins lemon and lime.*

*The first Florida grapefruit grove was planted by the Frenchman Count Odet Phillipe in 1823.*

*The United States produces 90% of the world's grapefruit in Florida, California, Texas, and Arizona. Half of these crops are canned or made into juice.*

*Grapefruit are high in vitamin C, calcium, potassium, and fiber. Vitamin C helps fight certain viruses; increases the absorption of iron; lowers blood cholesterol; and helps in the treatment of cancer.*

*"Seedless" means, in fact, that a single fruit will not have more than five seeds.*

*The ugli, a new fruit on the market, is a cross between a grapefruit and a tangerine. Aptly named, it has an eery greenish hue and baggy skin. It is sweeter than a grapefruit and sharper than a tangerine.*

# GRAPEFRUIT
*Citrus paradisi*

The grapefruit, barely three hundred years old, is a relatively new species. It appeared rather mysteriously in Jamaica, where citrus fruits are not indigenous—having been introduced to the Caribbean by Columbus in the 15th century. Botanists are not sure if the grapefruit resulted from the crossing of two citrus fruits or a mutation of a single citrus species. Its ancestor is probably the pummelo (or shaddock)—a larger, less juicy fruit that originated in Asia.

In his book *Hortus Jamaicensis* (1814), John Lunan documented the new fruit and named it the grapefruit because, according to some sources, he thought its taste resembled that of grapes. Other sources claim the name stems from the fact that when the tree is heavy with fruit, it hangs downward in bunches like clusters of grapes.

The rather humble and glamorless grapefruit gained slow acceptance, and cultivation did not begin until sixty years after its discovery. Grapefruits were not popular in the United States until after World War I; in Europe, not until thirty years later. Today, they are the second most economically important citrus fruit after oranges. This is due in part to the fact that the trees require little maintenance, bear fruit early and abundantly, are resistant to frost, and adapt well to different types of soil.

> *A grapefruit is a lemon that had a chance and took advantage of it.*
>
> —ANONYMOUS

Despite public perception, growers and professional testers insist that there is no difference in sweetness between the pink and the white varieties. The food authority Waverley Root claims the pink variety was designed to suit the rather strange preference Americans have for colorful foods. Compared to all the luscious fruit available on the market, the grapefruit could only benefit from such a marketing tactic.

During the depression in the United States, grapefruits were traded for food stamps and introduced to many households for the first time. The Welfare Board received complaints from many housewives: after hours of boiling, the grapefruit still remained tough!

*Opposite, top: A small mountain of golden fruit frames Grapefruit Queen Marilyn Crane in Cypress Gardens, Florida.*

*Below, left: A cluster of grapefruit ready for harvesting.*

## RECIPE

### Candied Citrus Zests

Zests of 3 or more mixed citrus fruits
1 cup sugar
1 cup water
Superfine sugar
Melted chocolate

Remove the zests with a zest stripper and cut into 2-inch-long strips.

In a saucepan, boil the sugar and water over low heat until the sugar dissolves. Add zests and simmer for 15 minutes or until they turn transparent.

Remove zests with a slotted spoon and put them on a bed of sugar. Cover the zests with the sugar and leave them to dry.

Melt chocolate in microwave, stirring every 30 seconds. Dip half of each zest into the melted chocolate. Store candied zests in airtight container.

# MELON
*Cucumis melo*

As its botanical name suggests, the melon of tropical Asia and Africa belongs to the cucumber family and so is related to squashes and gourds. These promiscuous vines crossbreed so readily that growers must plant different species at least a quarter of a mile apart to prevent unwanted hybrids. There are countless varieties of melons.

Melons must ripen on the vine, and because each variety and each fruit matures at a different pace, it is difficult to pick a perfect melon. The 17th century French poet Claude Mermet lamented:

> *Friends are like melons. Shall I tell you why?*
> *To find one good, a hundred you must try.*

Early texts and images of melons suggest that the fruit originated in Persia and has been cultivated and appreciated since antiquity. A Middle Eastern proverb reads: "He who fills his stomach with melons is like he who fills it with light; there is a blessing within it."

Melons were prized by the Romans, who imported the orange-sized fruit from Armenia, but they were not cultivated in Europe until the Middle Ages. By the early Renaissance, melons had become exceedingly popular; they were featured at every meal and eulogized in poetry and art. In France, melons were especially coveted. Professor Jacques Pons wrote a *Succinct Treatise on Melons* (1853) that listed more than fifty ways

## SIDELIGHTS

The watermelon, CITRULLUS LANATUS, is from a different botanical family than the melon, CUMIS MELO, and they do not crossbreed. Watermelons were cultivated in ancient Egypt.

The watermelon became an American favorite, and according to Mark Twain, "When one has tasted it, he knows what angels eat. It was not a southern watermelon that Eve took; we know because she repented."

**Right:** *Watermelon and Cantaloupe differ in the placement of their seeds.*

**Opposite, top:** *The beautifully mottled watermelon is synonymous with summer holidays in the United States.*

**Opposite, below:** *A colorful lithograph of the muskmelon and admirers.*

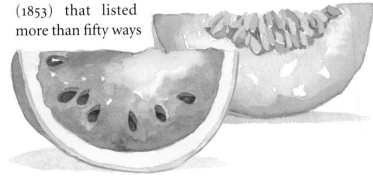

to consume the fruit. And when the town of Cavaillon, famous for its melons, asked Alexander Dumas, *pere*, for a complete set of his books (more than 400 volumes), the author stipulated that he receive a yearly shipment of Cavaillon melons in exchange.

*O precious food! Delight of the mouth!*

*O much better than gold, masterpiece of Apollo!*

*O flower of all the fruits! O ravishing melon!*

—MARC-ANTOINE SAINT-AMANT
*17th-century French poet*

Columbus introduced melons to the West Indies, where they flourished and spread so quickly throughout the New World that early settlers in North America believed the fruit to be native.

The name "cantaloupe" comes from the town of Cantalupo, near Rome, where the first melons were grown in Europe. Italians serve melon with paper-thin slices of prosciutto ham as an appetizer. The French serve small cantaloupes filled with port as an hors d'oeuvre, while the English sprinkle melon with ground ginger to bring out its flavor. The melon is the only fruit that is eaten at both the beginning and the end of the meal and is never cooked.

## RECIPE

*Melon Sorbet*
1 medium melon, cantaloupe or other
¼ cup water
¼ cup sugar
Juice of one lemon

In a saucepan, boil the water, sugar and lemon juice over low heat for 5 minutes. Cool. Purée melon in the food processor and mix approximately 2 cups of the purée with the cooled sugar/water syrup. Freeze in shallow pan or in ice-cube trays until almost solid. Purée the frozen mixture until the sorbet is light and smooth.

The sorbet may need to soften at room temperature. It is best if used within a day but will keep in freezer for several days. Garnish with candied citrus zests or fresh mint leaves.

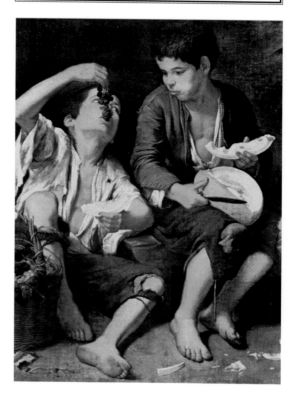

Mme. Tallien, prominent at the court of Emperor Napoleon I, had twenty-two pounds of crushed strawberries added to her baths in order to keep her skin smooth and soft. Strawberries are still found in cosmetics for conditioning skin and for whitening teeth.

In the Middle Ages, strawberries were used by alchemists for medicinal purposes; they were believed to be a general panacea. An infusion of strawberry roots and leaves has been used since the 18th century to treat diarrhea.

In Norse mythology, the fruit is special to the goddess of matrimony, Figga.

Strawberries and cream are wonderfully complementary, whether the cream is whipped, clotted, or créme fraiche.

To bring out the flavor of strawberries, sprinkle a few drops of good balsamic vinegar over the fruit.

It is traditional in France to serve newlyweds a soup of strawberries, sour cream, borage, and sugar.

# STRAWBERRY
*Fragaria family*

The sweet little wild strawberry has been enjoyed for centuries in Europe and the Americas by those who sought the fruit in the woods, where it grows abundantly under trees. The question thus arises as to whether it is necessary to improve upon nature. By the 1300s, wild plants were being transplanted for convenience into the gardens of the European aristocracy, as well as into family plots, but the plants were not cultivated. Attempts to improve the fruit were not made until there was a market demand for it. Despite cultivation, the European strawberry, *Fragaria vesca*, remained rather small and fragile until it was crossed with American varieties.

*Doubtless God could have made a better berry, but doubtless God never did.*

— DR. WILLIAM BUTLER
*17th-century English author*

The strawberry that we know and enjoy today is a hybrid descendent of the Chilean and Virginian varieties, *Fragaria chilonesis* and *virginiana*. Ironically, this crosscultivation did not occur in the Americas. An 18th-century French naval engineer and amateur botanist named Frézier brought the Chilean strawberry to his native west coast, where it was crossed with the American variety. Coincidentally, Frézier is pronounced like the French word for strawberry grower, *fraisier*.

The English word for this fruit may have been derived from the fact that the berries were brought to market strung on straw. Another source for the name is the Old English word *strew*, meaning stray, describing the way the vines branch off from the main plant.

From medieval times, recipes have combined strawberries and wine, and today, strawberries and champagne are a popular duo with alleged aphrodisiac attributes. The Roman senator Cato (234–149 BC) so loved strawberries soaked in wine that he inspected his own plants every morning for the concoction.

Strawberries are not, in fact, a true fruit, which is defined as a seed surrounded by flesh. In fact, the fruits of the strawberry are embedded on its surface. Called "achenes," each of them is a fruit with one seed. Because of the many tiny seeds, the strawberry is regarded as a symbol of fertility.

FROM
### Chilean Strawberry/ Wild strawberry

*. . . Frutilla*
*of earth and heaven*
*sweet juicy*
*and sometimes sour*
*you spring up*
*unexpectedly,*
*but never at the wrong time,*
*like a prayer*
*or a candle*
*to delight the taste buds*
*of candid people*
*those who*
*still wear*
*a basket of stars*
*on their foreheads.*

— MARJORIE AGOSIN
*Chilean-born poet*

**Opposite, top:** A Feast of Strawberries, *E. H. Stannard.*

**Left:** *The Alpine strawberry.*

# ℬLUEBERRY
*Vaccinium family*

Growing abundantly in North America, the blueberry was a favorite food of several Native American tribes. Early colonists readily adopted the fruit, and images of New England summers came to be almost synonymous with the joyous ritual of gathering blueberries. Henry David Thoreau described blueberry-covered mountaintops, Robert Frost wrote a poem about picking them, and Winslow Homer painted children in straw hats collecting them along the rocky coast.

---

*Blueberries as big as the end of your thumb,*
*Real sky-blue, and heavy, and ready to drum*
*In the cavernous pail of the first one to come!*
*And all ripe together, not some of them green*
*And some of them ripe! You ought to have seen!*
— ROBERT FROST, *American poet*

---

## SIDELIGHTS

*The United States and Canada grow 95 percent of the world's commercial crop, with over 200 million pounds harvested annually.*

*Bigger is better with blueberries. Although for most fruits size does not affect flavor, in the case of cultivated blueberries (as with Bing cherries), bigger berries are more flavorful.*

*Blueberries are high in vitamin C and fiber.*

*Blueberries are bacteria-fighting and can help cure urinary tract infections.*

The low-bush blues, *Vaccinium augustifolium*, are wild plants that grow from one to two feet high along the New England and Canadian coastline. The berries must be harvested by hand, and much of the fruit is canned, frozen, or dried. Recently, these wild blues have been so much in demand that landowners hire guards to protect them from thieves stealing into the patches at night.

Until the early 20th century, there was only the low-bush blue. Eventually, cultivation was rewarded by the common high-bush blueberry, *Vaccinium corymbosum*, and its near relatives, the Southern rabbit-

eye blueberry (*Vaccinium asher*). The cultivated varieties are larger, brighter in color, and have smaller seeds than wild blueberries. Moreover, high-bush blueberries grow up to sixteen feet and can be harvested mechanically. Today, it is the high-bush varieties that dominate the commercial market.

The journal of explorers Lewis and Clark described a Native American dish that included smoked venison with blueberries pounded into the meat. Native Americans ate the fruit fresh or dried. They also used the roots for tea and made a blueberry syrup consumed to relieve winter coughs. Blueberries were called "starberries" because of the star-shaped calyx on each berry where the blossom forms.

The bilberry, a relative of the American blueberry, grows wild in northern Europe. American blueberry plants were imported in its stead, because they are larger, sweeter, and easier to pick than the bilberry.

When buying blueberries, look for those with a waxy, white dusting. This dusting, called "bloom," is nature's way of protecting the fruit from the sun. The bloom fades after harvesting, and the darker the berry, the longer it has been since it was picked.

*Above:* Winslow Homer's Berry Pickers *brings a New England summer vividly to mind.*

*Opposite, below:* Ripe *blueberries with the characteristic "bloom" that protects them from scorching by the sun.*

# GRAPE
*Vitis vinifera*

O lder than recorded history, the grape is deeply symbolic, especially in the form of its most celebrated by-product—wine. Grapes have played an essential and sacred role in religious rituals throughout the millennia. In art and literature, the grape motif has represented pleasure and plenty.

Fruits have traditionally represented fertility, rejuvenation, and abundance, and grapes are pre-eminent. For Christians, red wine symbolizes the blood of Jesus Christ, while the grapevine's branches represent his disciples, and the fruit, the faithful; for some Eastern mystics, wine signifies divine love, wisdom, and truth; and for Jews, grapes symbolize peace and plenty. In antiquity the god of wine, Dionysus (Bacchus), was associated with fertility, art, and, of course, intoxication. He was honored by frequent festivals where the elixer flowed freely and his followers engaged in acts of hedonism.

Instructions for grape and wine production appear in ancient Egyptian hieroglyphics, and the tomb of Tutankhamen contained a jar with the inscription "unfermented grape juice." But it was the ancient Romans who spread the knowledge of viticulture throughout continental Europe and into England. No fewer than ninety-one varieties of grapes, and fifty different wines are cited by Pliny, the Roman naturalist. In antiquity, a sugar syrup made from grapes was the principal sweetener, while verjuice, made from unripened grapes, was a souring agent in use before vinegar or lemon juice. In Europe, during the Middle Ages, viticulture was developed extensively by monasteries, where wine was used for religious ceremonies and medicinal purposes, as well as for enjoyment.

*Always eat grapes downward — that is, always eat the best grape first; in this way there will be none better left on the bunch, and each grape will seem good down to the last. If you eat them the other way, you will not have a good grape in the lot.*

— SAMUEL BUTLER
*17th-century English poet*

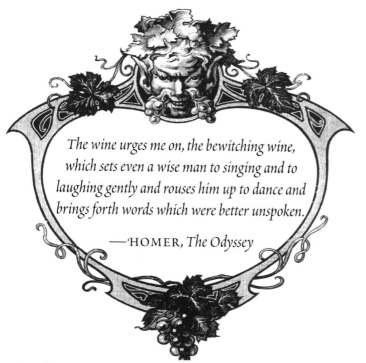

*The wine urges me on, the bewitching wine, which sets even a wise man to singing and to laughing gently and rouses him up to dance and brings forth words which were better unspoken.*

—HOMER, *The Odyssey*

Various varieties are developed specifically as dessert grapes, for wine, or for raisins. Good wine grapes are determined by the proper balance of acid and sugar. Wine is made by fermenting the grapes through a

process which allows the yeast to convert the fruit's sugar into alcohol and carbon dioxide. When making sparkling wine or champagne, the gas is contained, creating the bubbles. It was in the 18th century that champagne became the wine of choice for celebrations.

The development of raisins is over 4,000 years old: they were probably the result of a heat wave that dried the grapes still on the vine. The Israelites used raisins to pay taxes to King David in 1000 BC. The word raisin is derived from the Latin *racemus*, which means a bunch of grapes. Mediterranean currants are, in fact, dried Black Corinth grapes, while sultanas are dried Thompson Seedless grapes.

When Lief Erickson, the Norse explorer, reached the North American continent in AD 1000, he discovered such an abundance of wild grapes that he called the area "Vinland." After unsuccessful attempts to transplant grape vines from the Old World, the American colonists began cultivating the wild native grapes. However, European varieties were well suited to California's climate, and by the late 18th century West Coast vineyards were well established. American rootstock, resistant

to the parasitic insect that decimated most European vineyards in the late 1800s, was used for replanting throughout Europe.

---

## "Beulah, peel me a grape."

— MAE WEST, *I'm no Angel* (1933)

---

Grapes have unusual therapeutic qualities and are especially good for the kidneys; they help eliminate waste and excess acids. They are also a good source of vitamin C and potassium. Grape cures—or "ampelotherapy"—were a feature of the fall harvest during the 18th and 19th centuries and involved eating nothing but grapes and drinking only grape juice as a purifying treatment.

---

### R E C I P E

*Catsou's Frosted Grapes*
2 egg whites
Grapes in small bunches
Superfine sugar

Lightly beat the egg whites until foamy. Dip washed and dried grapes in the egg white. Shake off excess and coat the grapes in the sugar. The grapes will dry in an hour with a sparkling crust. The grapes can be eaten on the day of preparation (caution: uncooked egg whites may contain harmful bacteria) or used for decoration.

---

**Opposite:** *(top) A 16th-century French tapestry showing the winemaking process; (below, left) Mural from the tomb of Nakht at Thebes, where wine was left as a sacrificial offering.*

**Right:** *A Victorian Tribute to Bacchus, artist unknown.*

*Above: Market in Martinique, West Indies.*

*Opposite, top: Advent of refrigerated rail transport.*

*Opposite, below: Botanical drawing, 1880.*

---

### RECIPE

**Banana Flambé**
4 bananas, peeled and split lengthwise
Generous amount of butter
Brown sugar
½ cup rum or brandy

In a large heavy skillet, brown both sides of the bananas in butter over low heat. Sprinkle the brown sugar over the bananas and add the rum or brandy. Quickly remove from heat and carefully ignite with a match.

For a more elegant presentation, put the browned bananas on a warmed serving plate, pour warmed rum or brandy over the bananas and then ignite.

---

# BANANA
### *Musa sapientum*

The banana is believed to have originated in India and Malaysia more than 4,000 years ago. As with so many foods from the Far East, bananas first traveled westward with Arab traders; later, 15th century Portuguese and Spanish explorers brought them to Europe. The fruit reached the New World in 1516 with the Spanish missionary Tomás de Berlanga.

---

*The leaf is like birds' wings. The fruit . . . is delightful for the sweetness of its juice.*
— PLINY, THE ELDER, 1st century AD

---

Bananas were known in the United States as early as 1850, but they remained a luxury until the advent of steamships with sophisticated refrigeration. These "banana boats" were designed with climatized compartments so that the green fruit could ripen en route from the tropics. Two American entrepreneurs began the international banana trade when they founded the United Fruit Company in 1899. The company wielded tremendous influence throughout Central America, where the countries that became dependent on the trade were known pejoratively as "banana republics."

Although treelike in appearance, the banana is the world's largest plant without a woody trunk: it is, in fact, an herb. Wild bananas are seedy and inedible. The edible cultivated types are seedless because they are sterile. Each stem bears fruit only once and

then is cut down. New stems from the same root system perpetuate the plant's life.

The botanical name *Musa sapientum* is attributed to Alexander the Great, who encountered wise men (*homines sapientes*) with bananas in India. De Candolle wrote that "sages reposed beneath its shade and ate of its fruit." The European name comes from the West African Guinean word *banema*.

A cousin to the sweet yellow banana is the larger plantain, which must be cooked and is eaten as a vegetable. Plantains are a staple food in many places and are delicious mashed, fried, baked, or boiled.

The fruit is most widely employed in Eastern countries like India, where it is a good complement to hot and spicy foods. Bananas are also fermented to make beer and dried to make banana chips.

## Legend

A Hindu legend identifies the forbidden fruit eaten by the first man and woman as a banana. Paradise was the island of Sri Lanka, and the couple's nakedness was covered by banana leaves, which can grow to twenty-six inches wide and as long as five to twenty feet long—surely much more effective for this purpose than fig leaves.

## SIDELIGHTS

*Bananas are an excellent energy food with high levels of carbohydrates, potassium, and vitamins B and C.*

*Today, the United States is the largest importer of bananas: Americans eat more than twenty-five pounds per person per year.*

*An especially delicious combination is dates with dairy products. In Arabian cuisine, dates are often served with buttermilk or butter, while the French stuff the dates with a bit of unsalted butter, and Indian recipes often pair cream and dates.*

*There are over 60 references to the date palm in the Old Testament, and it is identified as the Tree of Life in Genesis.*

*The name date comes from the Latin word* DACTYLUS, *meaning "finger," which the short brown fruit resembles.*

# DATE

*Phoenix dactylifera*

The date palm tree and its fruit, the date, has been indispensable in the daily lives of many North African and Arabian people for centuries. The date itself contains enough sugar, potassium, calories, iron, protein, phosphorus, and vitamins to sustain the nomadic lifestyle of the desert, while the tree yields other products of economic value. The stems and leaves are used to thatch huts, and to make hats, rope, mats, and baskets. In an area where firewood and building materials are scarce, the wood of the trunk provides valuable timber. The date palm seeds are pressed for oil or roasted into coffee, while the buds, called hearts of palm, are also edible.

The tree grows over 100 feet tall, providing essential shade from the desert heat. It is symbolic of an oasis, because the date palm tree signals the existence of ground water below. The Moslem fasts of Ramadan are always broken by eating a date, and Muhammad told his followers to "cherish your father's sister, the [date] palm tree."

*It's never too late*
*To succumb to a date that's plump*
*    as a camel's hump*
*And far sweeter than an old Potater.*
— ANONYMOUS

Date palms originate from the Persian Gulf and were cultivated in the Sahara during Neolithic times—one of the first trees to be grown by humankind. The cultivation of dates is a true labor of love.

The female plants must be pollinated by the male plants, and because the male flower emits no scent to attract insects, natural pollination relies on the wind. In order to ensure pollination without forfeiting too much land for the non-fruiting male trees, workers must climb the seventy-five-foot male tree, gather the pollen, then climb the equally tall female tree and blow the pollen onto the female pods.

The tree bears fruit after four years, with the greatest yield at eighty years. Eventually, the tree may produce in such abundance that it dies: unable to support its own weight, it topples over.

Date palms require very specific growing conditions in order to fruit. Temperatures must stay between 70° and 92° Farenheit, and there must be enough water for the roots but no humidity near the leaves at the top. For this reason, the date palm is described as having "its feet in the water and its head in the sun."

**Opposite, below:** *Date palm, seedling, and cutaway sections of the fruit.*

**Above and right:** *A bearing tree, and dates for sale in an Israeli market.*

### SIDELIGHTS

*Arabic names for the many varieties of dates are highly descriptive. A fine, delicate variety is called "bride's finger," and a pear-shaped, coarse-skinned variety is called "mule's testicles."*

*Dates, called "finger apples," were well known in Medieval Europe.*

# Fig

*Ficus carica*

"I call a fig a fig, a spade a spade," wrote Menander, the ancient Greek playwright. That would make it appear simpler than it is—there are more than 750 species of figs and their nomenclature is unclear, as the same fig may be grown in several neighboring regions and called by a different name in each.

Figs grow on vines, trees, underground, in the desert, and in tropical forests. They vary in shape, and in color they range from black to white. One thing they all have in common is a high sugar content, which renders any type of fig deliciously sweet.

The fig tree is one of the oldest cultivated plants. Although originally from Turkey, figs have been an important food staple throughout the Mediterranean for centuries, along with dates and apricots.

Baskets of figs, as well as writings about them, were found in ancient Egyptian tombs. The ancient Greeks' love for the delicate fig is well known, and the fruit is mentioned in their literature. Pliny, the Roman naturalist, described a fig tree planted in the Roman forum in memory of the original tree under which the twins Romulus and Remus were suckled by a she-wolf. That tree was worshipped, and during the Bacchus festivals, women of the city wore necklaces of figs as symbols of fertility. Figs have long been associated with fertility and female sensuality, perhaps because the flower, with its many seeds, grows within the fruit and the luscious pulp surrounds it.

## SIDELIGHTS

The word SYCOPHANT, a self-serving flatterer, dates to ancient Greece and means "fig shower." A sycophant was someone who gained favor with authorities by reporting fig smugglers.

"Giving the fig" in Mediterranean countries involves an obscene gesture with the thumb.

The pear-shaped fruit is eaten fresh or dried. Unfortunately, fresh figs are delicate and not often available outside the region where they grow.

Figs have more dietary fiber than prunes, broccoli, and bran and more potassium than bananas. They are also high in vitamins A, B, and C.

The fig is a member of the Mulberry family.

The flower is contained within the fruit, and is the anatomical inversion of the strawberry.

There are numerous references to figs in the Bible, the most well known being in Genesis when Adam and Eve cover their nakedness with fig leaves. Throughout art history, depending on the climate of propriety, fig leaves have been used to cover nakedness in sculpture and painting.

For Hindus, the fig tree is significant because their god Vishnu was born under such a tree. The holiest of all fig trees grows in the ancient city of Anuradhapura in Sri Lanka. The tree grew from a cutting of the Holy Bo tree, *Ficus religiosa*, under which Buddha achieved enlightenment. In Islam, the fig tree is regarded as the Tree of Heaven since this is where Mohammed pledged a sacred oath. The fig is the symbol of Israel and represents peace and plentiful supply in Judaism.

Figs spread from the Mediterranean whenever trade routes opened. They were introduced to Europe, but were not commonly available in northern Europe until the 16th century. Figs reached the New World at about the same time and were established in the hospitable climate of California by Franciscan missionaries. Although most fig trees are self-pollinating, the oldest cultivated fig, the Smyrna, is not. When introduced to California in the late 1880s, it was necessary to import the male trees and the fig wasps (not bees) that are essential in fertilizing the female fruit-bearing tree.

---

*Now sing of the fig, Simiane,*
*Because its loves are hidden.*

*I sing of the fig, said she,*
*Whose beautiful loves are hidden,*
*Its flowering is folded away*
*Closed room where marriages are made:*
*No perfume tells the tale outside.*

— ANDRÉ GIDE, *20th century French poet*

---

**Opposite, top:** *The Buddha enthroned beneath a royal fan of figs.*
**Opposite, below:** *Cutaway section showing the fig's internal flower.*
**Above:** *Coypel's image of the fig leaf as artistic convention.*
**Below:** *Fig gatherers in ancient Egyptian art.*

## SIDELIGHTS

*The unspecified fruit of the Tree of Life growing in the garden of Eden is thought by some scholars to have been a pomegranate.*

*Long before the introduction of paper and ink, the indelible red juice of the pomegranate was used by Egyptians to write on papyrus. The juice was also used as a fabric dye.*

*The explosive called a grenade was named after pomegranates, whose shape they resemble.*

*The pomegranate is nicknamed the Christmas apple because when red and fully ripe, it resembles a Christmas tree ornament.*

*Pomegranates are rich in phosphorus and potassium, with some vitamin C.*

*For centuries, the pomegranate tree has been planted next to other plants in order to ward off pests. Recently, agriculturists have begun to use pomegranate extract as a natural pesticide.*

# POMEGRANATE
## *Punica granatum*

This ancient fruit originated in Persia (Iran), but it has long been popular in eastern Mediterranean regions and the Near and Far East. The unusual fruit resembles no other in its structure: it is shaped like a rounded hexagon with leathery skin ranging in color from brownish-yellow to red. The interior membrane is honeycombed with hundreds of bright red jewel-like kernels. The kernels are juicy and each contains a large white edible seed.

In the Middle East, pomegranates have long been appreciated for their thirst-quenching ability and sweet-tart flavor. Ancient Egyptians made wine from fermented pomegranates, and dried seeds were used as a condiment. Today, Middle Eastern cuisine often features the juice as well as the seeds. Although a seedless variety had already been developed long ago, and small-seeded pomegranates are cultivated in Afghanistan, many enjoy the crunchy seeds and the juice that can be pressed from them.

Europeans, however, usually use the fruit on the table for decorative purposes, cut in half to embellish a fruit basket, since few consider the small amount of juicy pulp worth the effort to extract it. The fruit was used medically until the Renaissance, when recipes featuring the pomegranate began to appear. Today, central Europeans use the pomegranate mostly for its juice, to make jellies, sorbets, and the popular French syrup called *grenadine*.

The pomegranate, with its seemingly infinite number of seeds, is a symbol of fertility in many cultures. The traditional Turkish bride throws down a pomegranate and counts the number of seeds that fall out, believed to indicate the number of children she will bear. In Ancient Greece, married women celebrated the goddess of agriculture, Demeter, with a festival in October. One day of the festival was devoted to fertility and featured the pomegranate. Chinese women wishing for children offer the pomegranate fruit, as well as porcelain decorated with pomegranate designs, to the goddess of mercy. Sephardic Jews enjoy the pomegranate at Rosh Hashanah, the Jewish New Year. A many-seeded pomegranate means the family will be blessed with many children in the years to come.

## Legend

In ancient Greek legend, the goddess Persephone, who was the daughter of Zeus and Demeter, was kidnapped by Hades and taken to the underworld. Demeter, goddess of agriculture, was so distraught that she neglected the harvest and the fruitfulness of the earth, which resulted in famine. She appealed to Zeus and won Persephone's release on the condition that she eat nothing in the underworld. But Persephone was unable to resist the pomegranate and ate six seeds. She was condemned to spend six months of each year with Hades in the underworld. The other six months she was permitted to return to the world of sunshine and life. The myth symbolizes the earth's springtime release from winter's darkness.

*Below:* Detail from a pomegranate border in a Book of Psalms (c. 1870).

FROM *Pineapple*

*Mixture of spurs*
*fragrant and thick*
*full of yellows*
*pleasing on the tongue bright*
*    and dark*
*you are offering*
*and sign*
*of welcome*
*and before Mr. Columbus*
*you were supreme,*
*reigning over regions*
*from Antigua*
*to majestic Chavín*
*in the Peruvian peaks...*

— MARJORIE AGOSIN
*Chilean-born poet*

**Right:** *Harvesting this prickly fruit requires thick gloves and protective sacking between basket and bearer.*

**Opposite, below:** *The pineapple centers this welcoming door-lintel display.*

# ᔔINEAPPLE
## *Ananas comosus*

Although it originates in Brazil, this fruit was already well established when Columbus found it in the West Indies. Its discoverers called it a "pineapple" because it resembled a large pine cone and tasted like a sweet, juicy apple. Fifteenth-century Portuguese sailors kept an ample supply of pineapples aboard; the fruit kept well over long periods and provided the much-needed vitamin C to prevent scurvy. In fact, sailors are said to have spread pineapples to Africa and India, since the plant takes root easily from discarded foliage in a sufficiently warm climate.

The pineapple gained immediate popularity when introduced to Europe, where growing the fruit became fashionable among the wealthy—so much so that its cultivation there is said to have contributed to the development of the greenhouse. King Louis XI, however, banned the cultivation of pineapples in France after cutting his lips on the prickly skin—in his greed and impatience he had bitten into the fruit before it had been peeled.

## The princess of fruits.
— SIR WALTER RALEIGH

By the 18th century, pineapple motifs began to appear in the decorative and fine arts, in coats of arms, in furniture, and in tapestries. In domestic architectural ornamentation, the pineapple carved into a gate or above a doorway symbolizes hospitality—a tradition derived from Native Americans, who hung pineapples over entrances as a sign of welcome.

The fruit found its ideal home in Hawaii in the 18th century: the climate and soil there are suitable for cultivating pineapples. Today they comprise Hawaii's major fruit crop, and the Islands can claim the world's most flavorful variety. However, it wasn't until modern transportation and refrigeration that fresh pineapples from Hawaii were widely available in the marketplace.

The pineapple has been lauded in print: Sir Walter Raleigh called it "the princess of fruits," while an early European enthusiast described it as having "a delicious taste which combined the flavors of melons, strawberries, and pippins." The same writer declared it "one of the best fruits in the world." Jean de Lery, a Brazilian incorrectly credited with discovering the fruit, was even more rhapsodic about the pineapple when he claimed, "the gods might luxuriate upon it and it should only be gathered by the hand of a Venus."

## SIDELIGHTS

*The Spanish named the fruit* PIÑA, *since it resembles a large pine cone, while the French call it* ANANAS, *from the Brazilian Indian word meaning "excellent fruit."*

*The largest producers include China, Hawaii, Southeast Asia, Central and South America.*

*The plant takes two to three years to flower. Each plant grows one large pineapple and several smaller ones once the large fruit is harvested.*

*Because the fruit has a high sugar content and no starch reserves, it will not ripen after it is picked and should be eaten soon after harvesting. For the most flavorful pineapples, look for a tag that indicates the fruit has been flown in from Hawaii.*

# VEGETABLES

VEGETABLES ARE DEFINED AS ANY EDIBLE plant or plant part—a definition that could include any number of species. The vegetables chosen for this book are those commonly used in kitchens across Europe and North America. Of the seventeen listed here, eleven are, in fact, fruits, while the artichoke is a flower, and mushrooms are neither fruit nor vegetable, but fungi. It is because they are savory that these plants are described and used as vegetables.

Unlike fruits, most vegetables are high in vitamins, minerals and carbohydrates—a compensation, perhaps, for their lack of glamor vis-à-vis the colorful fruit family. For most of the world's people, the high-protein, easily grown grains and legumes, such as the bean, potato, pea, and corn, are indispensable, as they comprise the staple diet. Many a cuisine is centered around the versatility of the eggplant (or aubergine), the spiciness of the chile pepper, or the reliability of potatoes, while entire economies have been built on corn and olives. 🐛 🐛 🐛 🐛 🐛

*Page 50:* Malmesbury Market, *by the English artist H.C. Bryant (fl. 1860–80).*

## SIDELIGHTS

*Squash are fruit of the*
CUCURBITACEAE *family. They*
*are an annual herbaceous plant*
*whose fruits are berries, and they*
*bear unisex flowers on each plant.*

*Squash comes in a multitude of*
*shapes, colors, and sizes. Some of*
*the winter squashes are enveloped*
*by skins so warty, rough, and*
*irregular that they belie the delicious*
*pulp within.*

*The word squash is from the Native*
*American* ASQUATASQUASH,
*"eaten raw or green," referring to*
*summer squash, which*
*is often eaten uncooked.*

# SQUASH
*Cucurbitaceae family*

The Native American dietary triad referred to as the "inseparable sisters" includes squash, beans, and corn. Squash were unique to America, where they have been cultivated for over 9,000 years. They were unknown in the Old World until Spanish explorers returned with them in hand. Gourds, on the other hand, are native to Africa and Asia and were introduced to the Americas by the same Spanish explorers. Although most gourds are dried for use as containers, musical instruments, or decorative items, some varieties are also eaten as well, leading to considerable confusion between squashes and gourds. Squash is the generic American

name and includes squashes, gourds and pumpkins; the British equivalent is "vegetable marrow." For culinary purposes, squash is divided into two groups—winter and summer squash.

Summer squashes are mild in flavor and tender. Because they are eaten in their entirety—skin, seeds, and all—they should be cooked when immature. Summer squashes grow quickly, are somewhat fragile, and are best eaten soon after harvesting. Popular summer squashes include the yellow straightneck and crookneck, the British custard marrow, and the zucchini, which is also called a *courgette*. The zucchini is of Italian origin, and the unopened flowers are delicious when sautéed or deep fried.

Characteristics of the winter squash include a tough outer skin, irregular shape, and orange pulp and seeds that are removed and prepared separately. Winter squash are traditionally harvested in late autumn and can be stored for several months. They are considerably more nutritious than their summer counterparts, with a high carbohydrate content. Popular winter squashes include the acorn, butternut, Hubbard, and, of course, the legendary pumpkin.

***Opposite, below:** A romantic depiction of a frontier harvest.*

***Below:** Both summer and winter squashes have prickly leaves and stems.*

*Pumpkins,
immense,
gigantic,
round like the bellies
of wise women
with children
or without them,
pumpkin,
golden
burnished by the spectra
of the wheeling sun.*

— MARJORIE AGOSIN
*Chilean-born poet*

### Pumpkin

Pumpkin is the general term for large, orange winter squashes central to fall harvest traditions. They feature prominently in children's literature and are an American favorite to carve at Halloween into jack-o'-lanterns intended to keep evil at bay.

In the story of Cinderella, her glamorous coach turns into a pumpkin at midnight; in Charles Shultz's comic strip *Peanuts*, Linus awaits the arrival of "the Great Pumpkin"; and in a nursery rhyme, Peter, the pumpkin eater, keeps his wife in a pumpkin shell.

In China, where pumpkins symbolize fruitfulness, health, and enrichment, they are nicknamed the "emperor of the garden."

Pumpkins grow in large, open fields on vines: their name is derived from the Greek word *pepon* meaning "cooked by the sun."

Growing pumpkins competitively has long been a popular pastime. At the 1900 World's Fair in Paris the winner was a 400-pound pumpkin. Recently, entrants in such competitions have weighed in at over 800 pounds!

The ancient Mayans used pumpkin sap for burns, and several Native American tribes knew that the seed could relieve kidney infections and kill intestinal parasites. By the mid-19th century, pumpkin seeds were a known diuretic and cure for worms. Chewing pumpkin seeds has long been a folk remedy for prostate problems, and recent studies prove the practice to be effective.

It is the sugar pumpkins that are used to make the delicious dessert pie traditional in the United States and an equally popular savory pie in northern France.

## Legend

A variation of the Biblical deluge story, told in India, centers on a sage named Iaia. When his son fell sick and died, Iaia placed him in a hollowed-out pumpkin and left the pumpkin at the foot of the mountain. Some time later, Iaia opened the pumpkin and out came fish, and even whales, followed by water. He mentioned the event to four brothers of his village, and they went to see the pumpkin hoping to catch fish. When they accidentally broke the shell, rivers began to flow incessantly until the earth was covered with water. Eventually, these waters formed the oceans.

Jack-o'-lanterns on Halloween are a Celtic tradition of the British Isles. Jack is a legendary folk figure who was excluded from heaven for being so wicked and expelled from hell for outwitting the devil. Condemned to walk the earth forever, he filled a large turnip with coals from hell to light his way through dark nights. Large turnips were traditionally hollowed out and lit by a candle to keep the evil spirits away on the last day of the pagan calender, October 31. When the custom came to the New World, pumpkins were substituted for the turnip.

***Above:*** *Halloween is one of American children's favorite holidays, with its costumes, candles, and jack o' lanterns.*

### RECIPE

*Pumpkin Soup*

1 29-ounce can puréed pumpkin
2 strips bacon, chopped (optional)
1 large onion, coarsely chopped
Olive oil
½ cup walnuts, coarsely chopped, toasted in the oven or microwave
½ cup sherry
4 cups vegetable stock
Salt and pepper to taste
1 tbs. grated ginger
1 cup buttermilk

Sauté the onions and the bacon in olive oil in a large soup pot. Add the remaining ingredients, except buttermilk.

Simmer until the flavors blend. Add the buttermilk, stir and serve.

# CUCUMBER
*Cucumis sativus*

**Opposite, top, and below:** *Slices of cucumber show the edible seeds, which add to the texture of Middle Eastern dishes prepared with yogurt and spices.*

**Opposite, below:** *Among the first of the H.J. Heinz Company's famous "57 varieties" was this blend of sweet pickles, onions, cauliflower, and pimento.*

The expression "cool as a cucumber" comes from the fact that the interior of a cucumber can be as much as twenty degrees cooler than the outside air. Cucumbers contain up to 96 percent water—almost as much as their cousin the melon. The cucumber's thirst-quenching and cooling qualities have long been appreciated by those living in hot climates. Believed to have been cultivated in India over 3,000 years ago, the plant spread west and east from there.

*Ah, my cucumber, the cucumber gives us a cool mind and we all know the importance of keeping the mind cool. Right from my childhood I've been extremely fond of you and this fondness will last forever.*

— SRI CHINMOY, *Hindu spiritual leader and poet*

The many-seeded cucumber has signified fertility in many cultures and, because of its shape, was also a phallic emblem. A Buddhist legend tells of Sagara's wife, who had 60,000 children. The first offspring was a cucumber, whose descendants climbed to heaven on his far-reaching vine.

The Hebrews cultivated cucumbers in Galilee, and when they had left Egypt to spend two years in the desert, they sorely missed the refreshing plants: "And the children of Israel also wept again….We remember…the cucumbers." (Numbers 11: 4-5) The ancient Greeks and Romans also relished cucumbers; the Romans even made wine from them. The Roman emperor Tiberius insisted on having them at his meals every day, year-round. His slaves carted movable hotbeds around to follow the path of the sun.

Aside from its cooling properties, the cucumber's popularity would seem improbable, since it has negligible food value. Cucumbers contain no fat, no fiber, no sodium, no cholesterol, and only negligible amounts of vitamins and minerals. Moreover, many people find the cucumber indigestible, inducing flatulence. So while the plant was revered by people from hot climates, many in the temperate zones empathized with Dr. Samuel Johnson, the 18th-century encyclopedist, who made the following suggestion: "A cucumber should be well sliced, and dressed with pepper and vinegar, and then thrown out, as good for nothing."

## SIDELIGHTS

*Cucumber juice has long been used in cosmetics for softening and whitening the skin. The French cultivated a white variety solely for cosmetic purposes.*

*Cucumbers were also used medicinally to cleanse the blood and soothe coughs.*

*A more digestible cucumber, called "burpless," was developed by the Japanese.*

*Pickled cucumbers followed soon after fresh ones. They were considered good for the stomach, as the vitamin A content increases during the pickling process, making them more digestible.*

*Sunbeams may be extracted from cucumbers, but the process is tedious.*

— DAVID DAGGET, *19th century American legislator*

### Legend

In an ancient Japanese story, a tiny genie standing on a cucumber leaf spoke to a prince as he walked through his garden.

The genie proposed a bargain: he would protect the prince's family and all his descendants if they would agree not to eat cucumbers anymore. From then on, the cucumber was placed on the family crest and grown strictly for ornamental purposes.

## SIDELIGHTS

*In Europe, particularly in France, growers mound earth over the asparagus to block the development of chlorophyll in order to produce white asparagus. There is also a violet variety.*

*Thin asparagus are not necessarily more tender than the fatter spears. Tenderness depends, in fact, on the intensity of color — the better asparagus are the whitest of the white varieties and the greenest of the green.*

*Asparagus that are very fresh exude a little juice at the base when compressed.*

*According to the rules of etiquette, asparagus may be eaten with the fingers.*

*The Japanese cook the spears with sugar, while the Chinese candy them. Some cultures roast the seeds as a coffee substitute and ferment asparagus berries to make a drink.*

# ASPARAGUS
*Asparagus officinalis*

Little is known about the origin of the asparagus. The Egyptians offered bundles of asparagus to their gods. The ancient Greeks collected wild *aspharagos,* and by 2,000 BC, the Romans had begun cultivating the vegetable. Wild asparagus, very similar to its cultivated cousin, grows in sandy soil along riverbanks and in the forests of central Europe, western and central Asia, and northern Africa.

As with many foods that were familiar throughout the Holy Roman Empire, the asparagus seems to have disappeared in Medieval Europe. In the early 16th century, the plants were reintroduced to Europe and popularized by Louis XIV of France. The Sun King was so partial to asparagus that he demanded it even in December. The King's master gardener, La Quintinie, did, in fact, manage to satisfy his employer's craving by growing the plant in hotbeds.

The price of asparagus has always been, and still is, better suited to the king's purse than that of the average citizen. This, perhaps, is due to the fact that they must be harvested by hand and have very short

shelf life—ideally, they should be picked and eaten the same day.

The asparagus plant has a crown of underground rootstock that produces the young sprouts, or spears. If not harvested, the plant will produce feathery, fernlike leaves. Plants begin to yield after a few years, and will produce for ten to fifteen years or longer. During high season, the plants may grow as much as ten inches in a single day, requiring two harvestings daily.

Long before it reached the dinner table, the asparagus was used medicinally. The plant contains a substance called rutin that helps prevent small blood vessels from rupturing. Syrups from the plant have been concocted to cure heart palpitations and for use as a diuretic. The underground stems have been used to alleviate such diverse ailments as bee stings, toothaches, and venereal diseases.

> ## RECIPE
>
> ### Steamed Asparagus
> Snap off the woody bottoms of the spears. They will break naturally at the right point. The use of a vegetable peeler for the thicker bottom of the spear is optional.
>
> Bundle the spears with kitchen string and steam the asparagus standing upright in a pot filled with 3 to 4 inches of boiling water. This avoids overcooking the tips, which will disintegrate if overcooked. Bring the water back to a gentle boil and cook until the spears are tender, but still crisp.
>
> Drain well, and serve warm, or at room temperature, with melted butter, hollandaise sauce, or a vinaigrette.

*I stick to asparagus, which still seems to inspire gentle thought.*
—CHARLES LAMB, *19th-century English essayist*

## SIDELIGHTS

*Emperor Augustus preferred his asparagus cooked very quickly so that it would be slightly crunchy. Thus we have the expression* VELOCIUS QUAM ASPARAGI COQUANTUR, *"quicker than you can cook asparagus."*

*Strong-smelling urine results from eating asparagus due to a sulfur-containing amino acid in the vegetable.*

***Opposite and left:*** *Three views of the elegant and expensive asparagus: only a few of some 300 varieties, native mainly to Africa, are grown for food and foliage.*

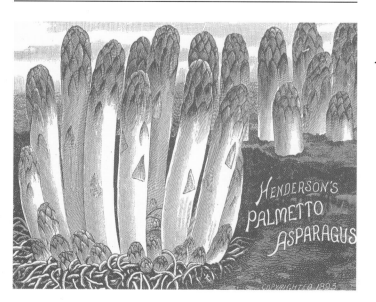

HENDERSON'S PALMETTO ASPARAGUS

COPYRIGHTED 1893

# CARROT

*Daucus carota*

Above: *This early 19th-century seed variety, Danvers Half Long, produced some 600 bushels per acre and was recommended for feeding stock.*

Opposite, top: *Giuseppe Arcimbolo's whimsical painting* The Vegetable Man.

Below: *Contemporary tastes dictate a longer, slimmer carrot.*

It is difficult to imagine that the carrot, today one of the most widely available and least glamorous of vegetables, was once considered exotic. Carrots held the limelight briefly during the reign of King James I, when English ladies of the court wore the feathery greens of young carrots in their hats and pins.

## Only in dreams are carrots as big as bears.

— YIDDISH SAYING

The ancient root was not always treated with such reverence. Although the Greeks and Romans did eat the vegetable, it was neither greatly relished nor cultivated. As with so many fruits and vegetables, the carrot was originally used medicinally. The ancient Greeks used the plant to relieve stomach ailments and to increase virility. Its Greek name, *philon,* from the word *philo,* "to love," reflects the fact that carrots were eaten prior to lovemaking.

Iranian men of the late 1800s also believed in the aphrodisiac qualities of carrots and ate them stewed with sugar to help increase the quality and quantity of sperm. One might wonder whether the carrot was considered aphrodisiac because of its obvious phallic shape, or because of its association with rabbits and their reputation for procreation.

*The carrot is a member of the parsley family.*

*A large amount of carotene is converted into vitamin A in the liver, with benefits to eyesight. Carrots are high in sugar and rich in vitamins B and C.*

*Through cultivation, the tough, woody center has been minimized; the best varieties have no fibrous center.*

*The American wildflower Queen Anne's Lace is an offspring of carrots that escaped cultivation to revert back to their wild form.*

Our English word is derived from the Latin *carota*, "to burn," undoubtedly referring to the bright-orange variety. Carrots do, however, vary in color, ranging from yellow to red and even purple. Some Asian types have round purple roots that resemble beets. The bright- orange carrot common today was developed in Holland in the Middle Ages.

The root is actually a native of Afghanistan, but was cultivated in the Mediterranean long before Christ. Europeans knew of the root by the 13th century, but it was not widespread until the 16th century. Cultivated carrots were introduced to the New World by the colonists and were enthusiastically adopted by many of the native peoples.

# ᛈEA

*Pisum sativum*

Of the hundreds of pea varieties, the two main cultivated types—the field and garden peas—could not be more different. Whereas the ancient field pea is a very pedestrian staple food, the garden pea, a relatively new variety, is associated with images of spring, harvesting and shelling the tender pea, and enjoyment of the garden's earliest vegetable during its very short season.

Garden peas, also called "green peas," were practically unknown before the 16th century. The Italians developed the new peas, *piselli novelli*, which are eaten immature, raw, or slightly cooked. *Piselli novelli* were introduced to France by Catherine de Médici, and the French eagerly adopted the young, tender peas. Their popularity soon spread throughout Europe and the Americas, where they remain a particular favorite. Peas signal springtime as they are the first to appear in the vegetable garden. Limited availability increases the allure of this tiny, ephemeral vegetable.

Jane Grigson, the food writer, laments the ubiquity of the inferior frozen garden pea and writes: "I should like to go back in time to the great days of the garden pea, and invite myself to dinner with Thomas Jefferson .... I would choose late spring for my visit, when everyone

**Right:** *Ripe peas in the pod.*

**Opposite, top:** *A nostalgic portrait of a farmer's wife shelling peas by W.K. Blaylock, early 20th century.*

**Opposite, below:** *An 1893 advertisement from the catalogue of Peter Henderson & Co, agricultural suppliers.*

was waiting to see who would be the first to put peas on the dinner table."

---

*At court, the pea saga still continues. The desire to eat them, the pleasure of having eaten them and the joy of eating them again are the three topics which our princes have dwelt on for the past four days.*

— MADAME DE MAINTENON
*17th century French marchioness*

---

She continues by recounting a story in which growing and serving the season's earliest garden peas was a competition among Jefferson's friends in the vicinity of Monticello, Virginia. Every year, the winner was the same — Mr. George Divers, whose reward was to host a dinner featuring these first peas. One year, however, it was Jefferson's own peas that appeared first. Rather than strip Divers of the honor, and bruise his friend's pride, Jefferson, with his family, held a clandestine dinner to celebrate spring's very first peas.

Unlike the garden pea, the field pea is so ancient that its exact origin is unknown, although it is believed to have spread from western Asia. Field peas were cultivated in Europe from very early times and were known to Greeks and Romans. Because they can be dried and stored, peas have long been an important staple food, especially for the working class:

> Pease Porridge Hot,
> Pease Porridge Cold,
> Pease Porridge in the Pot,
> Nine Days Old

This Mother Goose children's rhyme sums up the ubiquity of the field pea, which was eaten all too often. So does the old English saying: "Love and pease porridge are two dangerous things; One breaks the heart and the other the belly." But as dull as the dried pea may be, its importance as a staple food throughout history for many peoples cannot be overlooked.

### Legend

While shelling garden peas, it is folkloric custom for a young unmarried woman to keep an eye out for a nine-pea pod. The rare pod is put upon the door lintel, and the first eligible male who enters will be the one she marries.

**SIDELIGHTS**

*The most prominent families of ancient Rome were named after beans — Fabius is from the faba or fava bean; Lentulus from the lentil; and Cicero from the chick pea, because an ancestor had a wart on his face shaped like this bean.*

*Legumes are the mature seeds that grow inside pods of beans and peas and are dried for use.*

*Beans are so ancient that the word is synonymous with seed and is akin to the Sanskrit verb "to eat."*

*In ancient Rome, a prayer to one's ancestors involved the head of the family throwing nine beans over his shoulder nine times.*

# Bean

*Leguminosae*

The humble legume has been an indispensable dietary staple for many cultures throughout history. Beans are high in protein, nitrates, iron, and phosphates, providing an excellent energy source when meat has been unavailable or undesirable. In many countries, beans have supplanted meat entirely. The versatile bean is eaten at every point in its life cycle — as sprouted seeds, as tender young pods, and as mature seeds, fresh or dried. Although there are seemingly infinite varieties and sub-varieties of beans, the following kinds are especially noteworthy.

The American **haricot**, *Phaseolus vulgaris*, also called the "common bean," is a native of southwestern Mexico, where it was first cultivated over 7,000 years ago. As it spread north and south, the bean adapted to the varying climates by developing new varieties. There are now more than 500 varieties in an incredible range of shapes, sizes, and colors. They include the black bean, string bean, yellow eye, marrow, navy, pinto, pigeon, black-eyed peas, and many more. The haricot was introduced to Europe by Spanish explorers returning from the New World and became the most widespread bean on the

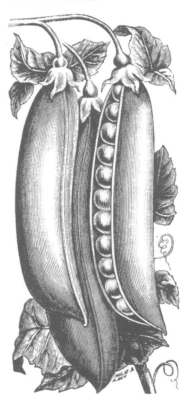

Continent. Today, the French champion the haricots, which are often called "French beans."

The **Lima** bean, *Phaseolus lunatus,* named after the capital city of Peru, predates the haricot bean. Native Americans planted these alongside corn, since the cornstalks offered the beans a natural pole to climb.

The **broad** bean, *Vicia faba,* is called the "fava bean" in the United States, while the English refer to it as the "Windsor" or "round bean." It had been a staple in Europe since the Bronze Age. Until the introduction of the American haricot bean, which eventually surpassed the broad in popularity, the broad bean was the only one known in Europe. Because of its resistance to drought, the broad bean is still common in North Africa and the Middle East.

**Lentils**, *Vicia lens,* originated in the Near East and are the oldest cultivated legume, dating to 7000 BC. The Bible tells the us story of Esau, who sold his birthright for a stew of red lentils. Most meals in India include *dahl,* a dish made of these beans. The double-sided convex glass called the lens was named after the similarly shaped lentil.

*Below: A purple-hulled legume with typical compound leaves. Many bean plants are climbers; others grow erect.*

*Opposite, top: String beans, often packaged as "French-style green beans."*

The **chickpea**, *Cicer arietinum*, is also known as "garbanzo," "gram," or "Egyptian pea." It is indigenous to the Mediterranean basin and is popular in Indian and Middle Eastern cuisine. The chickpea has been cultivated since 5000 BC — long enough so that no wild form of the plant exists today.

The Asian **soya** bean, *Glycine maxo*, is appreciated now not only as a food, but also for its many by-products: It is added to soil, fed to livestock, utilized in the production of glues, paints, and plastics. As a food, its versatility ranges from bean sprouts to soy flour, tofu, a milk-like beverage, and oil. Soya is so high in protein, it is often used as a meat substitute, especially in vegetarian parts of Asia. There are over 1,000 varieties. Although originally from China, today the biggest grower and exporter of soya beans is the United States.

*If rationality were the criterion for things being allowed to exist, the world would be one gigantic field of soya beans!*

— TOM STOPPARD, *Jumpers* (1972)

### Legend

Much negative lore surrounds the bean — as is often the case with food staples that are essential to the poorer classes. In the case of beans, it may be due, in part, to the deficiency disease favism, which is caused by eating too many broad beans at the expense of other protein sources, or to the indigestion and flatulence that may result from the consumption of beans.

Beans were said to induce insanity and nightmares. The privileged Greeks and Romans of antiquity thus avoided them, as did the oracles, for fear of losing divine revelations. The goddess Ceres would not accept beans as an offering or gift, and the Greek physician Hippocrates proclaimed that beans injured sight. In England, beans were placed in graves to keep ghosts away and were utilized in the exorcism of evil spirits. In Scotland, witches were alleged to fly about on bean stalks.

Occasionally, beans were given a more elevated status. Pythagoras, the Egyptian philosopher, believed that upon death, certain souls became beans. He would not eat them, since he believed that they were in part human. He died, in fact, while fleeing enemies who chased him into a bean field: To avoid trampling the beans, he stopped, and thus succumbed to his assailants.

At the English celebration of Twelfth Night, the recipient of the slice of holiday cake containing a bean is crowned king of festivities. This traditional custom dates back to the Roman era, when, during the feast of Saturnalia, the master of festivities was chosen by drawing beans.

## EXPRESSIONS

ABSTINETO A FABIS, *Latin for "abstain from beans," means to avoid politics. It dates back to the time when beans were used as ballots at elections and at court. A white bean indicated innocence and a black one, guilt.*

FULL OF BEANS *describes someone full of energy and/or spirit, and probably derives from the fact that beans are high in protein. It may also be because they cause flatulence.*

SPILL THE BEANS *means to have inadvertently disclosed a secret. The expression originated with gypsies, who told fortunes based on the way a handful of beans fell onto the ground.*

JUST BEANS *means unimportant information that is better ignored.*

NOT TO KNOW BEANS *refers to someone's stupidity or ignorance.*

BEAN COUNTER *refers to someone who works with numbers, as in accounting. It originated when beans were used as a counterweight for weighing gold.*

BEANFEAST, *in colloquial British, means any free party or celebration. It dates back to the 19th century, when employers offered an annual Christmas dinner, featuring beans and bacon, to all their employees.*

> *Of all the gifts of heaven to man, [the olive] is next to the most precious. Perhaps it may claim a preference even to bread. . .*
>
> —THOMAS JEFFERSON,
> *on the olive tree, which he tried unsuccessfully to grow in Virginia and North Carolina.*

# OLIVE

*Olea europaea*

**Above:** *A dove bearing an olive branch has long been the universal symbol for peace. The Bible recounts how Noah knew that the floods were receding when he saw the white dove returning with an olive branch.*

**Top right:** *Harvesting olives in Provence, from one of Van Gogh's last paintings at Arles.*

The deeply symbolic olive tree has been essential to the Mediterranean region since the tree's fruit became a food staple and its oil was pressed for cosmetics, perfumes, lamps, religious rites, and medicine. Cultivated before 4000 BC, the ancient olive tree is depicted in Egyptian art, while the olive, or *zai*, is the symbol denoting the fourth letter (after Alpha, Beta, and Gamma) in the Greek adaptation of oldest known alphabet—that of the Phoenicians.

When introduced to Greece, the olive tree flourished in the hot, arid climate and rocky soil that was inhospitable to most crops or animals. The olive tree provided the Greeks with needed fats for their diet and a valuable commodity for trade. The inhabitants of Attica relied heavily on the dependable crop, which is reflected in the legend of the capital city's name. A contest was held to select the city's patron god: the one bringing the most valuable gift would win. While both Athena and Poseidon competed for the honor, Athena won easily when she struck her sword upon the ground and up sprang an olive tree in the Acropolis of what is now Athens. The olive was sacred to Athena, the goddess of learning, because the oil was burned in lamps and symbolized knowledge. The olive tree also stood for victory, and at the ancient Olympic games, the first prize was an olive wreath.

Because olive trees live as long as 300 to 600 years, the plant came to symbolize longevity, and the Greeks and Romans frequently rubbed olive oil into the skin to ensure good health and a long life. Olive oil was used medicinally; in fact it contains salicylic acid, the active ingredient in aspirin.

The ancient symbolism of the tree preceded its culinary uses in northern Europe, and in 1598 Shakespeare wrote in *Henry IV*:

*There is not now a rebel's sword unsheath'd,*
*But peace puts forth her olive everywhere.*

Although essential to Mediterranean cuisine and culture, the olive was little known outside the area where it was grown until after the European Renaissance. Today, Spain is the world's largest producer of olives and their oil for reasons that date back to the 8th century. When the Moors ruled, the prohibition of pork and pork fat led to a wider use and greater production of olive oil. The two other major producers are France and Italy. Olive trees were introduced to the New World by Spanish explorers in the 15th century. They still flourish in Mexico and California.

> *"There are two liquids especially agreeable to the human body, wine inside and oil outside"*
> — PLINY, THE ELDER, 1st century AD

Olives are never eaten fresh: they must be cured first. European olives are ripened on the vine, after which they are brine-cured or oil-cured. American olives are picked green, but some are oxidized and marketed as black, or "ripe," olives. Moroccan olives are dry-cured, and Greek olives, which many consider the tastiest, are cured by dry salt or brine.

## SIDELIGHTS

*The categorization of olive oil into virgin, extra virgin, fine and superfine refers to the oil's free oleic acid content. The finest oils are a product of the first pressing made by a cold-pressing method.*

*90% of the world's olives are made into oil.*

*The olive is high in sodium, is 18% oil by weight, and gets 85% of its calories from mono-unsaturated fats.*

*Olive oil is rarely used in Asian cooking, although it has been known in the Far East since the 6th century.*

**Above:** *This illustration from a Mediterranean vase of the 6th century BC shows the traditional method of gathering olives by flailing the tree with long poles.*

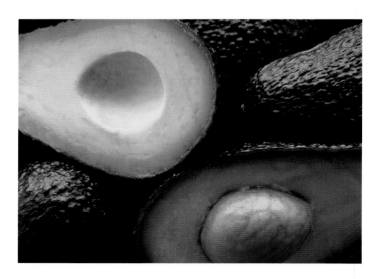

## SIDELIGHTS

*A single tree averages 500 fruit, but some can produce up to 2,000. It takes nine months for the avocado to mature on the tree.*

*The fruit begins to ripen only once it has been picked.*

*The different varieties of avocado range in weight from a few ounces to three pounds and come in many shapes and sizes, from round to pear-shaped with a long, slender neck*

**Above:** *The avocado seed can be rooted in water to grow an attractive houseplant.*

**Below:** *A member of the laurel family, the avocado tree is usually trimmed low in cultivation for ease in picking the fruits.*

# AVOCADO
## *Persea americana*

The avocado, a fruit, originated in tropical America, probably in Mexico. Whereas other tree fruits are either sweet, tart, or sweet-tart in flavor and have juicy flesh, avocados have a unique bland flavor and a dense, butter-like texture. Because of the low water content, the flesh is high in nutrients, particularly minerals and the B vitamins. Avocados are higher in potassium than bananas, high in mono-unsaturated fats, low in sugar and sodium. Although it is a fruit, the avocado's high oil content is similar to that of a nut.

The name "avocado" is the Spanish conquistador's version of the Aztec word *ahuacatl*, which means "testicle"—a reference to the shape of the fruit, which grows in pairs. Other names for the avocado include "alligator pear," since some varieties have rough skin; "avocado pear," because of its shape; and "midshipman's butter," by the English, since it was taken aboard ships for the petty officers. It is a "poor man's butter" in the tropics.

Although the returning Spanish explorers introduced the avocado to Europe in the early 16th century, the fruit does not propagate easily, and the avocado was scarce in Europe until after World War II. Israel began growing the fruit commercially in its hospitable climate, and today supplies the majority of the European market.

In many countries, the avocado is a staple and is most often eaten as a vegetable, either raw or cooked. It is sometimes served for dessert with sugar and lemon, or made into ice cream, as is done in Brazil. In Zaire, a beer is brewed from avocado leaves.

## Legend

A South American legend accounts for the constellations Orion, the Pleiades, and the Hyades. Seriokai and his wife lived in the forests of Guiana, where the husband's favorite fruit, avocado, grew abundantly. A hoglike tapir came to his hut by night and stole his wife's heart. She severed her husband's legs and fled with her lover.

Bent on revenge, Seriokai pursued them as soon as he could travel. He tracked the adulterous couple by following the avocado trees that had grown from the seeds his unfaithful wife discarded as she and the tapir fled. The trees became smaller and younger along their path until they were saplings, and Seriokai knew that he was close to finding the two. Finally, there were no trees, only avocado seeds, and there he found the lovers.

As Seriokai shot an arrow at the tapir, the animal leapt off the edge of the world, and Seriokai's wife followed him. Seriokai ran after the lovers and still pursues them across the sky. He is the constellation Orion, his wife is the Pleiades, and the tapir, the Hyades, with one bloodied eye where an arrow found its mark.

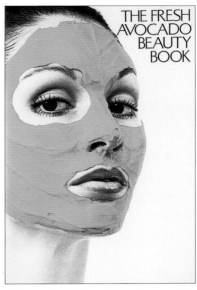

THE FRESH AVOCADO BEAUTY BOOK

**Above:** *Avocado oil is often used in cosmetics for its moisturizing qualities. The West Indies, Israel, and tropical America are the main sources of the fruit.*

## RECIPE

*Guacamole*
2 ripe avocados
1 plum tomato, seeded and chopped
1 small red onion, chopped
1 chile pepper, minced
1 garlic clove, minced
dash of Tabasco
juice of one lemon or lime
chopped cilantro, salt and pepper to taste

Mash the pulp of the avocados, add all ingredients and serve at room temperature with blue corn chips and margaritas.

## SIDELIGHTS

*Marilyn Monroe was crowned the first Queen of Artichokes in 1947.*

*The choke — the vegetable's fuzzy center — is actually an immature flower surrounded by leafy scales. If left to bloom, it will produce a beautiful cluster of purple flowers.*

*The artichoke is a thistle and related to the sunflower.*

*Artichokes are rich in vitamins B, A, C, calcium, iron, and potassium.*

*The Italians make an aperitif from artichokes called* CYNAR, *which aids digestion.*

*In selecting artichokes, look for tight leaves and no discoloration at the top of the scaly leaves.*

*Although the most familiar variety is the Globe, there are many artichoke varieties and sizes, some of which are small and are eaten whole — choke and all.*

*In France, the vegetable was first used only medicinally for the elderly and for those suffering from melancholy.*

# ARTICHOKE
*Cynara scolymus*

The artichoke may have earned its reputation as an aphrodisiac for several reasons: its rich nutty flavor, the fact that it must be eaten with the fingers, or the labor of love required to get to the tender, prized heart of an artichoke. Native to the western and central Mediterranean, the artichoke has been known and enjoyed for over 2,500 years. It has been cultivated, however, only since the 15th century.

---

*The artichoke above all is the vegetable expression of civilized living, of the long view, of increasing delight by anticipation and crescendo. No wonder it was once regarded as an aphrodisiac.*

— JANE GRIGSON, *British food writer*

It was widely used in southern Italian cooking when Catherine de Médici married Henri II, heir to the French throne, in 1533. Catherine brought with her Italian chefs who introduced many new foods to France, including the artichoke. Her fondness for the vegetable created a scandal and was the talk of France: she was, after all, only fourteen when she showed such an appetite for the alleged aphrodisiac.

Despite claims by the town of Castroville, California, to be "Artichoke Capital of the World," Italy is unquestionably the largest producer and consumer of this food, followed by Spain, France, and Greece. The Italians, in fact, eat 200 times as many artichokes as the Americans do. However, Castroville's claim is legitimate in that some of the tastiest artichokes originate there, in the cool foggy climate that is ideal for growing them.

---

*These things are just plain annoying.*
*After all the trouble you go to, you get about as*
*much actual "food" out of eating an artichoke as*
*you would from licking 30 or 40 postage stamps.*
*Have a shrimp cocktail instead.*

—MISS PIGGY

Artichokes contain cynarin, an acid that enhances the ability of taste buds to discern sweetness. Therefore, food often seems to taste sweeter after eating artichokes. The fact that cynarin does not affect everyone indicates that the susceptibility to it is very likely to be genetic. Because of the effect of cynarin, wine connoisseurs will often avoid artichokes on a menu that includes very fine wine.

## RECIPE

### Steamed Artichoke

Cut off the stems and snip off the prickly tips of the scaly leaves with scissors. Stand the artichokes in a covered pot containing an inch of salted water. Boil gently for 30 to 45 minutes until the bottom leaves are easily pulled off and tender. The water may need to be replenished. Drain the artichokes well before serving. The stems may be steamed and eaten, too.

Serve the artichoke hot with a pot of melted butter or a hollandaise sauce, or serve at room temperature with a vinaigrette.

### How to Eat an Artichoke

Eating an artichoke may seem daunting to those trying it for the first time, but it is really quite simple. Starting at the bottom of the artichoke, pull the leaves off one by one, dipping the pale bottom into the sauce. Gently pull between the teeth, scraping off the tender flesh at the base of the leaf. The leaves become more tender as one nears the center. Eventually, the entire leaf can be consumed. Carefully remove the fuzzy choke with a knife, leaving intact the heart. There is the prize—the mouthwatering heart. Enjoy!

**Opposite, top:** *Artichokes in the field at Castroville, California, showing their long prickly leaves, and, below, in cross-section.*

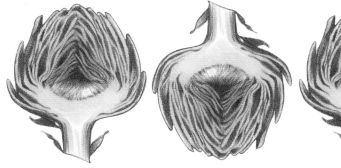

# ONION

*Allium cepa*

**Above:** *An 18th-century Spanish still life of onions, leeks, and shallots (artist unknown). These vegetables are still integral to Spanish cuisine, with its many pungent regional variations.*

**Opposite:** *The sweet red onion is especially popular for use in salads and as a garnish.*

The pungent and tangy onion grows wild throughout the world, and has been cultivated for over 5,000 years. In antiquity, the easily gathered and grown vegetable was a staple for the poor. Onions were relegated to the underprivileged only until the Middle Ages, when they became popular with people of all classes. This food is a culinary essential in so many cultures, one is hard pressed to fathom preparing a meal without first chopping an onion.

*It is hard to imagine a civilization without onions.*

— JULIA CHILD, *American chef*

To the ancient Egyptians, the onion symbolized the universe. In Egyptian cosmology, heaven, hell, and earth were concentric, like the layers of an onion. The sacred vegetable was a common offering to the gods, and paintings representing onions, as well as onions themselves, were found in Egyptian tombs.

---

*The onion brings to the kitchen of the cities a little of the countryside . . . . The onion offers always, and especially in the winter, a little of the springtime of the soil, preserved in its bulb.*

— RAYMOND DUMAY, *French author*

---

It was not infrequent that the slaves who constructed the great pyramids were compensated with onions. These were very sweet—because onions grown in warm climates are sweeter and milder than those grown in temperate climates—and were eaten raw, like an apple.

As a symbol of eternity the onion is a traditional form for church domes in Russia and Eastern Europe. The onion-shaped dome was believed to ensure the structure's durability and longevity.

The onion's seemingly endless layers have also been compared to superficiality. Henrik Ibsen's protagonist in the play *Peer Gynt* is derided:

"You're no Emperor. You're just an onion. . . . What a terrible lot of layers there are! Surely I'll get down to the heart? No—there isn't one! Just a series of shells."

All onions contain varying amounts of sulfurous oil. Some even have enough to induce tears from the most stoical people, as well as upset stomachs. The oil is also

## SIDELIGHTS

*An ancient Turkish legend recounts that when Satan was cast from heaven, garlic sprouted where he placed his left foot and onions where he placed his right.*

*Onions are rich in vitamin C, sulfur and mineral salts. In naval history, they were rationed to sailors to prevent scurvy.*

**Right:** *Detail from an earth-toned still life by Gauguin.*

**Below:** *An old gardener's catalogue offers a variety of "long-keeping" onions.*

**Opposite, below:** *Traditional onion-shaped domes on a Moscow cathedral.*

responsible for the bulb's legendary odor. Much of this dissipates, however, in cooking, which inspired Jonathan Swift, the 18th-century Irish wit, to write:

> There is in every cook's opinion,
> No savory dish without an onion:
> But lest your kissing be spoiled
> The onion must be thoroughly boiled.

Onions have an antiseptic agent that has long been used medicinally. A raw onion halved and slightly warmed was traditionally applied to burns and bee stings. Onions were once hung in rooms where people congregated in order to draw any purported diseases that might otherwise inflict the people gathered there. They also induce perspiration and have been used by those suffering from congestion and colds.

*How easily happiness begins by
dicing onions. A lump of sweet butter
slithers and swirls across the floor
of the sauté pan, especially if its
errant path crosses a tiny slick
of olive oil. Then a tumble of onions.*

—WILLIAM MATTHEWS
*American poet*

## Legend

An old Christmas custom alludes to St. Thomas, to whom the onion was sacred. An unmarried woman would cut an onion in half and whisper the name of the man she wished to marry. Holding the onion over her head, she prayed:

> *Good Saint Thomas do me right,
> and send my true love come to-night,
> That I may see him in the face,
> and him in my kind arms embrace.*

If the young woman was in bed by midnight, she would have visions of her future husband and their wedding.

*Onion skin very thin,
Mild winter coming in.
Onion skin very rough,
Coming winter very tough.*

— TRADITIONAL RHYME

### RECIPE

*French Onion Soup*
4 large yellow onions, thinly sliced
3 tbs. butter
Olive oil, as required
2 tbs. flour
½ tsp. sugar
8 cups beef or mushroom broth, warmed
½ tsp. thyme
Salt and pepper to taste
Dash of cognac or port
6 slices of French bread, toasted
Shredded Swiss or Gruyère cheese

In a large soup pot, sauté the onions in the butter and cook over low heat for 30 minutes. Stir frequently and add oil as required. Add the sugar to help caramelize the onions.

Sprinkle the flour over the onions. Stir. Add broth, thyme, salt and pepper. Cook for 20 minutes over low heat.

Divide the soup into individual crocks. Add the dash of cognac or port. Float the bread on top of the soup, sprinkle generous amounts of cheese, and bake in a preheated 400° F oven until the cheese is melted.

## SIDELIGHTS

*Garlic belongs to the lily family and is closely related to shallots, leeks, and onions. The plant grows twelve inches high and produces delicate white flowers. The bulb, or head, grows below ground and contains eight to ten sections called cloves. Each clove is wrapped in thin, papery membrane.*

*The word garlic is Anglo-Saxon and means "spear leek." The name refers to the plant's vertical shoots, which resemble a spear, as well as the bulb, which resembles the head of a spear.*

*Dogs love garlic. It is a common ingredient in dog food.*

*Sulphur of allyl, a component of garlic, is known as an aphrodisiac. The French king Henri IV, famous for his sexual exploits, was rumored to have been baptized with garlic.*

# GARLIC

*Allium sativum*

*What garlic is to salad, insanity is to art.*

—AUGUSTUS SAINT-GAUDENS,

*19th-century Irish-born American sculptor*

Few are ambivalent about garlic: the intensely pungent bulb is either relished or reviled on one's plate. Medicinally, however, no one doubts garlic's long-standing renown as an antiseptic, antibiotic, and a stimulant.

Aristophanes' claim that garlic lent courage and banished lethargy led athletes to eat it prior to exercising; Pliny insisted it cured consumption; the prophet Muhammad said it relieved the pain of snake and scorpion bites; and English herbalist Culpeper believed it was a panacea. Garlic has been used to cleanse the liver, gall bladder, and the respiratory system; to treat malaria; and to prevent tuberculosis and dysentery. Externally, it has been used to help cure pimples, lip cancer, hemorrhoids, earaches, and athlete's foot.

In fact, young garlic contains allyl disulphate, an antiseptic oil that inhibits the growth of bacteria. It is no surprise that the bulb used to prevent disease was an invaluable device in keeping away other reapers of death—vampires, the evil eye, and witches.

During the English Great Plague of the mid-1600s, all the residents of one house in Chester stayed healthy while thousands died around them. Their good health was attributed to a cellar full of garlic. In the early 1700s, Marseilles, France, suffered a devastating plague. Four thieves caught robbing corpses were offered amnesty for their crimes in exchange for their secret to good health in spite of contact with the dead who had succumbed to the plague. They wore masks soaked in garlic vinegar. In America, as recently as 1918, people wore garlic garlands to prevent illness during the influenza epidemic.

The bulbous plant probably originates from Central Asia, but garlic spread throughout the world long ago. It has been cultivated in China for more than 6,000 years, and it was widely used by the Egyptians, Greeks, and Romans. The ancients appreciated garlic as a vegetable and ate it whole, rather than as a seasoning for other foods.

# Garlic is the catsup of intellectuals.

—ANONYMOUS

Garlic was introduced to Europe initially by the Romans, and imported by returning Crusaders who had learned of it in the Middle East. It was widely accepted for its medicinal attributes, while others valued its culinary features. Before refrigeration, garlic conveniently masked the unpleasant odors of aging meats: therefore it was generally more widespread in warmer climates. The use of garlic is a mainstay of Middle Eastern and Southern European cuisine.

*Opposite: Garlic's renown as a deterrent to creepy creatures was enhanced by such horror movies as* Vampires of Prague, *with scary Bela Lugosi as the "Lord of the Undead."*

## RECIPE

### Aïoli
Aïoli, said to have been invented by Emperor Nero, is known today as the "butter of Provence." It has been enjoyed for centuries, but the reader is strongly cautioned that raw egg yolks may contain bacteria that can seriously endanger health.

4 large garlic cloves
2 egg yolks
Salt and pepper to taste
½ cup of olive oil
½ cup of vegetable oil
1 tbs. lemon juice

Put the garlic and egg yolks in the food processor. While blending, slowly add the oil and blend until it is the consistency of mayonnaise. Add lemon juice, salt and pepper and blend until mixed.

"Aïoli epitomizes the heat, the power, and the joy of the Provençal sun, but it has another virtue—it drives away the flies."
  — Frédéric Mistral
  *Founder of* L'Aïoli *magazine (1890s).*

# MUSHROOM
*Agaricus family*

All mushrooms are fungi, but only half of the 100,000 species of fungi are actually mushrooms. Of these, 2,000 species are eaten, only thirty-two are toxic, and fewer than ten are deadly. But it is those few that led the Roman philosopher Seneca to declare "Voluptuous poison!" while Emperor Nero designated mushrooms a "food for the gods," since few mortals could hazard the risk of eating the delicacy.

The paradoxical mushroom has long been saddled with evil as well as virtuous associations. While it is prized for its meaty texture and delicate flavor, the mushroom has also been widely feared because of the potentially deadly effects of some varieties. So intriguing is the malevolent mushroom that it has been featured in the writings of Hippocrates, Keats, Diderot, Tennyson, D.H. Lawrence, and Emily Dickinson.

One of the most primitive wild foods, mushrooms have long been gathered and eaten. Because they require a specific, lightless environment, mushrooms were not successfully cultivated until the 17th century, by the French. Today, only twenty of the eighty commonly eaten varieties are available commercially in France. In the United States and Great Britain, only the *Agaricus bisporus* are widely available, but this is rapidly changing as demand for more flavorful varieties increases.

Mushrooms are not vegetables, as they do not produce chlorophyll, seeds, flowers or roots. They reproduce by disseminating tiny spores that issue from the gills in the form of dust and are carried to a hospitable environment for growth. The mushroom is, in fact, the "fruiting body" of the fungus, which remains underground.

The mythical toadstool usually refers to magical or poisonous mushrooms. Intoxicating and hallucinogenic mushrooms have been used by Native Americans of many tribes and by Vikings for ceremonial purposes. In Mexico the mushroom signifies knowledge and enlightenment, while the Chinese believe mushrooms grow only during times of peace and are therefore symbolic of good leadership. In many cultures, mushrooms signify fertility and rebirth because of their rapid growth and reproduction.

## Legend

Pixie, or fairy rings, are mushrooms that grow in a circle formation around grassy meadows. The pixie ring of toadstools is said to be home to elves who dance in the meadows by night and crush the grass. If looked upon by these elves, one is advised to drink quinine to prevent the resultant fever. Similarly, a cow spied by an elf will produce sour milk.

The Scottish proverb "He who cleans the fairy ring an easy death shall die" discourages the disturbance of the sacred fairy rings. In fact, these "rings" spread outward centrifugally, extending the circle year after year as the young spores seek new feeding grounds with more nutrients. The crushed meadow grass is due to previous mushrooms that leave the underground fungi behind.

> *Overnight, very*
> *Whitely, discreetly,*
> *very quietly...*
> *We shall by morning*
> *Inherit the earth.*
> *Our foot's in the door.*
> — SYLVIA PLATH
> *British poet*

**Opposite, top:** *A 19th-century illustration of mushroom types.*

**Below:** *Edible mushrooms grown in California.*

# Potato
*Solanum tuberosum*

**Above:** *French peasants in a potato field pause for prayer in* The Angelus, *by Millet.*

There is no vegetable more historically important to Europe than this lowly tuber. However, its acceptance by some European countries, particularly France, was an arduous process. The potato is, after all, a member of the same family as the deadly nightshade, and a poisonous element, solanine, is found in flower, leaf, stem, and berries of the potato.

The potato originated in the Peruvian Andes, where the elevation was too high to grow corn. It was a staple of the Inca diet. Potatoes were cultivated for centuries before the Spanish explorers arrived in the early 16th century and brought the vegetable back to Europe. England and Ireland readily accepted the hardy and easily grown potato as a vital food crop. Potatoes provide more nourishment per acre than grain and will grow in poor soil.

*Be eating one potato, peeling a second,
have a third in your fist,
and your eye on a fourth.*

— IRISH PROVERB

For the French to overcome fears that potatoes caused leprosy, it took no less than the heroic efforts of A.A. Parmentier, the army pharmacist who had survived on potatoes as a prisoner of war during the Seven Years' War. Upon his return, he wrote a treatise on growing and cooking the vegetable that had saved his life. With the help of Louis XVI, who served the tuber at court, Parmentier promoted the novel food in France. He deceived suspicious peasants into trying the vegetable by posting guards around a potato field outside Paris. The peasants coveted the closely guarded crop and eventually raided the fields, initiating their first culinary experience of the potato.

***Below:*** *King Louis XVI visits the experimental potato field at the Sablons, near Paris, in an antique woodcut.*

## SIDELIGHTS

*The English name for potato is derived from the American Indian word* PATATA, *for sweet potato. The two vegetables were originally confused with each other, but the sweet potato belongs to the morning glory family and is not related to the common potato.*

*Although any potato can be mashed, the two best are Yukon Golds which have a creamy texture and rich buttery flavor and Russets which produce fluffy, light mashed potatoes.*

It is thought that the potato was first grown in Ireland on the estate of Sir Walter Raleigh in 1586. The plant was a godsend for the Irish who, continually at war, were frequently faced with famine. The potato spared the Irish from the famine of 1740, but by the time the potato blight hit Europe in 1845, Ireland had become a one-crop country. A succession of blights decimated Ireland's population: one million died, and thousands migrated to the United States during the "Great Hunger."

*What I say is that, if a fellow really likes potatoes, he must be a pretty decent sort of fellow.*

—A.A. MILNE, *20th-century English author*

During the 1774 famine in Prussia, Frederick the Great distributed potatoes to the starving peasants of Kolberg. They rejected the unfamiliar food until a soldier demonstrated how to prepare potatoes and ate the vegetable himself. Seventy-five years later, the potato was so much a part of German cooking that a statue of Sir Frances Drake with a potato in his hand was displayed. (Drake was erroneously credited with introducing the vegetable to Europe.)

---

FROM *"This Spud's for You"*

*Of solanum tuberosum, that vagrant vegetable, the Odysseus of tubers, the lumpy pill of the poor and starving, the shape-shifting and soothing potato, I sing.*

— WILLIAM MATTHEWS, *American poet*

---

**Opposite, top:** *Workers harvest the first potato crop in Ireland, allegedly planted on Sir Walter Raleigh's land in 1586. The food would become the mainstay of the Irish laboring class and even affected demographics: during the devastating potato blight of the mid-1800s, 2,000,000 emigrated from Ireland.*
**Below:** *The homely potato honored by Van Gogh.*

## RECIPE

*Mashed Potatoes —
The ultimate comfort food*

6 medium potatoes, preferably Yukon Golds or Russets, scrubbed and cut into small cubes
½ cup warmed lowfat milk
½ or more cup of reserved potato liquid
1 tbs butter
1 small garlic clove, crushed
¼ cup chopped fresh chives or parsley
Salt and coarse pepper to taste

Place cubed potatoes into large saucepan and cover with water. Bring water to a boil; cook potatoes over medium heat until tender.

Drain potatoes, reserving liquid, and return potatoes to the still warm saucepan. Add butter, milk, and garlic. Mash potatoes with a potato masher. Add parsley or chives, salt and pepper. Gradually stir in reserved liquid until desired consistency.

Less-than-perfectly mashed potatoes, fresh herbs and the potato skins give a nice texture.

*The eggplant is, in fact, a fruit but is prepared like a vegetable and is never eaten raw.*

*Not very nutritious, eggplants have a low energy value. They are, however, rich in potassium and calcium.*

*Eggplants belong to the nightshade family, which also includes pepper, potato, tomato, tobacco, and deadly nightshade.*

*The eggplant was introduced to the United States by Thomas Jefferson, but it never became popular. Even today, Americans eat only one eggplant per person a year.*

# ÆGGPLANT

## *Solanum melongena*

The eggplant (aubergine) is native to tropical Asia, and its Sanskrit name indicates that it was known in India since ancient times. No wild eggplant has ever been found—the vegetable is thought to be an improved or crossed form of various plants from India, and it has been cultivated for at least 4,000 years.

The Sanskrit name *vatin-ganah* means "wind go," and it is debated among food historians whether the word means that it causes or that it does not cause flatulence—this, to differentiate it from the other unsociable gas-inducing vegetables available at the time. As the plant traveled westward through Persia, Arabia, and Spain, the Sanskrit word evolved into the French and British name *aubergine*. The American name, eggplant, which was once used in Britain, comes from a small white egg-shaped type grown in the tropics.

The Arabs introduced the eggplant to Spain, where it was cultivated by the Moors. By the 16th century, eggplants were popular in Spain, where they were called "apples of love" and believed to be an aphrodisiac. At the same time, however, the eggplant was introduced to northern Europe as a decorative plant, accompanied by daunting tales of precaution, so that it was rarely eaten. Eggplants were called "mad apples" for their purported ability to inflict insanity, fever, and epilepsy. In 1597, Englishman John Gerald warned his readers in his publication *Herball* "…to content themselves with the meate and sauce of our owne country than with fruit and sauce eaten with such perill; for doubtless these apples have a mischievous quality; the use thereof is utterly forsaken."

The vegetable is a favorite staple in warmer climates, especially in the Middle East and Mediterranean. Middle Eastern Arabs claim over 1,000 ways to prepare it.

A well-known Turkish dish is called *Imam Bayildi*, which means "the Imam (Priest) fainted." It is said that when eggplants prepared this way were offered to a Muslim priest, he fainted with delight.

## Legend

Eggplant mixed with sea salt as a tooth-whitening solution comes from a Japanese legend. A beautiful young bride who sought to cure her husband of his unfounded jealousy made a paste from eggplant peel to blacken her teeth and make her less attractive. Later, when the eggplant mixture was rinsed away, her teeth were whiter than before.

## SIDELIGHTS

*They come in many shapes and colors — round, pumpkin-shaped, or long; thin or fat; white, green, yellow, red, purple, black, and combinations of the above.*

*Salting the eggplant flesh before cooking helps draw out the bitter taste and helps to diminish its sponge-like ability to soak up oil.*

***Above:*** *Italian Pink Bicolor Eggplant,* Solanum melongena.

***Opposite, top:*** *A variety of eggplants illustrated in* The Gardener's Assistant *at the turn of the century.*

***Left:*** *An early variety on the American scene, showing the plant's spiny stem and bushy lobed leaves.*

# PEPPER

*Capsicum family*

## SIDELIGHTS

*Peppers are related to the nightshade family, which includes tomatoes, potatoes, eggplant, and tobacco.*

*Although their vitamin C content varies, a pepper may have between two to nine times the vitamin C of an orange.*

*Peppers are high in potassium, fiber, folic acid, vitamin B-6, and vitamin E.*

**Opposite:** *The sweet red pepper is popular with home gardeners.*

**Below:** *The dried Cayenne chile can be used in sauces, soups, stews, including the popular dish chile,  and decoratively in wreaths and garlands.*

The pepper, or more accurately, the *chile* pepper, may have been simply called chile had it not been for Christopher Columbus's burning desire to find the source of the Oriental spice peppercorn. When he first discovered the chile in the Caribbean, he was, in fact, seeking *Piper nigrum*, peppercorn, which was highly coveted on the European market. Upon tasting the chile, dried and ground, he was convinced that he had found the pepper. In fact, *Piper nigrum* is a berry indigenous to Asia and is completely unrelated to the Capsicum pepper. Never mind: the Europeans were delighted to learn of a suitable peppercorn substitute that would grow on the Continent, and the misnomer persisted.

*In those islands there are also bushes like rose bushes which make a fruit as long as cinnamon full of small grains as biting as pepper; those Caribs and the Indians eat that fruit as we eat apples.*

— CHRISTOPHER COLUMBUS

Chile peppers had already been cultivated throughout the warm climates of the Americas long before Columbus arrived. They were among the earliest cul-

tivated plants, along with beans, corn, and squash. They were commonly used by the Incas, the Mayas, who grew more than thirty varieties, and the Aztecs, who ate chiles in almost every dish. Peppers crossbreed and spread easily and they were also grown by the ancient Native American pueblos of the south-west. Once they introduced it to Europe, the Spanish and Portuguese sailors spread the plant eastward along their maritime trading routes, and soon the pepper was cultivated worldwide. Mexico and India are the largest producers of pepper; chile peppers are an essential ingredient in Indian curries and in many Mexican dishes. The paprika pepper found a home inland in Hungarian cuisine, where today there is a thriving paprika industry.

For culinary purposes, peppers are usually divided into the large sweet peppers, *Capsicum annum,* and the smaller hot (chile) peppers, *Capsicum frutescens.* In general, the smaller the chile, the hotter the chile. The heat, or burn, associated with these peppers is caused by the capaicin concentrated in the white part to which the seeds are attached. Capaicin is the ingredient that is used in Mace-like sprays intended to fend off dogs and would-be attackers.

Chiles and their fiery heat have long been used in traditional medicine. In Mexico, a common cure for stomach problems includes eating a whole serrano chile. Other aliments aided by chiles include arthritis, bronchitis, epilepsy, malaria, parasite infes-tation, and toothaches. Capaicin, as any-one prone to eat hot chiles knows, is a natural decongestant.

## RECIPE

### Nonnie Mino's Peppers

3 red bell peppers, seeded and sliced in ½" wedges
3 cloves garlic, coarsely chopped
1 cup red wine vinegar
Extra virgin olive oil to taste
Salt to taste

Heat vinegar in large, heavy skillet. Add peppers and garlic. Cook on medium-high heat for 10 minutes or until fork tender. Toss frequently.

Remove peppers with a slotted spoon to a serving bowl. Add salt, and drizzle with extra virgin olive oil.

Allow the flavors to marry and serve them forth warm or at room temperature.

# TOMATO
*Lycopersicum esculentum*

## SIDELIGHTS

*The name tomato is derived from the ancient Mexican Nahuatl word* TOMATL.

*Tomatoes are a perennial herb related to the potato and green pepper. They are rich in potassium and vitamins A and C.*

*Salsa has surpassed ketchup as the most popular condiment in the United States.*

The tomato's Latin name translates into "wolf peach," a caveat signaling that while the fruit may be as appetizing as a peach, it is as lethal as a wolf. The French called the tomato *pomme d'amour*—"apple of love," like the forbidden fruit in the Garden of Eden. The Italians, the original tomato lovers, call the tomato *pomodoro*, "golden apple," after the original yellow tomato exported from the Americas.

The tomato is indigenous to the Andes, where it grows wild on long tree-climbing vines, bearing yellow, cherry-sized fruit. It was already widespread in Central America when the Spanish *conquistadores* arrived and eventually introduced the fruit to the Old World. Three hundred years later, the tomato was still shunned, shrouded by superstitions. Few outside Italy and Spain would eat its golden fruit, though many appreciated the tomato as a decorative plant. While the Italians were actively cultivating culinary varieties, the French still listed the

tomato as an ornamental plant in horti-cultural catalogues as late as 1850.

The very fruit that forms the basis of many great cuisines of Europe and the Mediterranean was once believed to be poisonous. Tomatoes were also thought to cause both gout and cancer. John Gerard, 16th century English herbalist, warned, "the whole plant is of a rank and stinking savour." The origin of the fear surrounding tomatoes is not exactly clear, but it may be linked to the fact that tomatoes, like all nightshade vegetables, contain a poisonous toxin, solanine, found in the plant's leaf and stem. These, however, have no culinary use, and in fact, tomatoes are now believed to contain anti-carcinogenic chemicals, while an antibiotic, tomatine, is extracted from the fruit's seeds.

## RECIPE

### Tomatoes à la Provençale

4 medium tomatoes
3 garlic cloves, crushed
Bread crumbs
Flat-leaf parsley, finely chopped
olive oil
salt and pepper

Cut tomatoes in half, from top to bottom. Gently remove excess seeds and juice. Sprinkle with salt and pepper.

Heat oil in heavy skillet and cook tomatoes, cut side down over medium-high heat, for a few minutes on each side. Transfer to an oiled baking dish, cut side up. Mix the garlic, bread crumbs, and parsley and sprinkle generous amounts over the tomato halves. Drizzle with olive oil and bake in preheated oven at 425° F until the tomatoes caramelize.

*I love them, the love apple. . . . The best way to eat them is in the garden, warm and pungent from the vine, so that one can suck unashamedly, and bend over if any of the juice escapes.*

—M.F.K. FISHER, *food and travel author*
*from* WITH BOLD FORK AND KNIFE

*Opposite, below* Still life with tomatoes and melons from The Gardener's Assistant *(1900).*

*Below:* Heinz Keystone Catsup was introduced by Heinz in 1876. The ketchup was thick, rich and spicy and at that time was considered the delicacy of condiments.

In the United States, Thomas Jefferson was the first to grow tomatoes. While the Spanish and the French settlers in Louisiana readily incorporated tomatoes into their cuisine, the Yankees were the last to accept them. Eventually, there was a considerable demand for the fruit and in 1893 tomato growers, in order to levy an import tax, petitioned the United States Supreme Court to officially list the tomato as a vegetable. Today, tomatoes are the third largest vegetable crop in the United States and the most widely used canned vegetable.

# Maize

*Zea mays*

FROM
## Maize/Corn

*Before words
and memory
before mosses and golds carpeted
    by fog
you appeared
enchanting, enchanted,
bringing summer's light
to the seasons . . .*

—MARJORIE AGOSIN
*Chilean-born poet*

Maize, also known as corn, has been the single most important food throughout the Americas—the cornerstone of many cultures and diets. For the Incas, the cultivation of maize instigated the crucial transition from a nomadic to an agricultural life style and accounted for their legendary prosperity. As the cereal grain was introduced north, many nomadic Native American tribes settled into agrarian communities. For this reason, the *Encyclopedia Britannica* describes maize as "the grain that built a hemisphere."

The fact that so many American tribes have legends, lore, and ceremonies featuring maize is testimony to its importance and sacred symbolism of plentitude and happiness. In several Native American languages corn is called "Our Mother," "Our Life," or "She Who Sustains Us." The word "corn" actually means cereal or grain. But since maize was the only indigenous food grain, it was known simply as "corn" and, in American

English, the name persisted. The word "maize" originates from the Arawak-Carib name *mahiz.*

---

*Sex is good, but not as good as fresh sweet corn.*

— GARRISON KEILLOR,

*From* ULTIMATE PRAIRIE HOME COMPANION

---

Although corn is nutritious, it alone is not a complete food because it lacks niacin. By combining what
the Iroquois called the three inseparable sisters—maize,
beans, and squash—the people formed a balanced diet.
Beans were planted next to the maize and grew up the
stalks, while squash was planted between the rows of
stalks to abate weeds. The medicinal uses of corn are
extensive: Native Americans used corn smut as a vaso-
constrictor and an antihemorrhagic, while corn byproducts served to cure ulcers, sores, dysentery, and bladder
and urinary disorders. Corn oil was used to relieve hay
fever, headaches, asthma, eczema, and dandruff.

**SIDELIGHTS**

*The adjective "corny," to mean old-
fashioned or maudlin, was a
reference to traditional rural
America as distinct from the
country's supposedly sophisticated
urban centers.*

*In the corn belt of the American
midwest, tradition dictates that
anyone who happens on a colored
ear of corn during a husking bee
may kiss the person of his choice.*

*Maize is rich in vitamin A,
thiamin, riboflavin, carbohydrates,
lipids, and proteins.*

---

*I believe in the forest,
and in the meadow,
and in the night which
the corn grows.*

— HENRY DAVID THOREAU

---

**Opposite, top:** *A photo-montage
from 1899 shows a colossal ear of
corn on a flatbed railroad car.*

**Left:** *Hauxtec farmers growing
corn in Mexico before the
European conquest.*

## DEFINITIONS

DENT CORN: *This hard yellow corn feeds livestock, and makes ethanol fuel, cornmeal, sweets, starches, corn oil, bourbon whisky, and beer.*

SWEET CORN: *This variety is eaten fresh on the cob, frozen, or canned. Fresh sweet corn is an American summer favorite. The corn should be eaten the same day as it is picked, since its sugar rapidly turns to starch.*

FLINT CORN: *This brightly colored variety is widely grown in South America, Central America, Asia, and Europe. It is hardy and resistant to disease and insects.*

FLOUR CORN: *One of the oldest types, this was an early American staple soft enough to grind into flour. The blue corn variety has recently regained popularity.*

POPCORN: *Although most dried corn will pop when heated, special varieties from Flint corn have been developed for this use. Popped corn was popular with the Iroquois, who used it for necklaces and ornaments as well as for eating.*

When early efforts by the American settlers to grow wheat in the New World failed, the colonists would surely have starved if not for the maize given to them by Native Americans. In Europe, maize was introduced early in the 16th century, but it has never been a popular food item. In Great Britian, sweet corn (as eating corn is sometimes called) has been increasingly accepted since the Second World War. The cereal was spread eastward by Portuguese traders and eventually reached China by the mid-16th century. Maize is a staple today in most of South America, parts of eastern Europe, and eastern and southern Africa.

---

*The corn is as high as an elephant's eye,*
*An' it looks like it's climbing clear to the sky.*
— RODGERS AND HAMMERSTEIN
*from the musical* OKLAHOMA! (1943)

---

Corn is a critical crop to the economy of the midwestern United States, which produces more than half of the world's harvest. Only ten percent of the world's corn supply is used as a vegetable; corn byproducts are used in or added to starches, sugars, ethanol fuel, corn oil, liquors, beers, sodas, plastics, cardboard, papers, textiles, leathers, and adhesives.

Maize must be cultivated. It does not reproduce itself because the seeds, or kernels, are enclosed by an impermeable shuck—those leaves surrounding the ear. Wild maize has never been found, indicating that the vegetable probably evolved from wild grasses called teosinte that still grow in the Mexican highlands. The widespread use of maize can be attributed to its remarkable variety and adaptability. It can be grown below sea level as well as in altitudes as high as 12,000 feet in the Peruvian Andes. Stalk sizes vary from two to twenty feet high and the ears vary from one inch to two feet long. Although white and yellow kernels are most common, they may also be red, purple, brown, blue, gold, or multi-colored. New colors are becoming increasingly popular.

***Opposite, below:*** *The corn shuck is pulled back to reveal the kernels surrounding the cob. Small whitish kernels are generally sweeter than the large bright-yellow ones.*

***Above:*** *An early-1900s label for canned corn grown in New England features an idyllic setting of meadow, stream, and children gathering flowers.*

*Lovely! See the cloud, the cloud appear!*
*Lovely! See the rain, the rain draw near!*
*Who spoke?*
*It was the little corn ear*
*High on the tip of the stalk.*

—ZUÑI CORN-GRINDING SONG

# ACKNOWLEDGEMENTS

The author would like to thank all the people who have made food and cooking fun—Maman, who wouldn't let her children leave home without knowing how to make a hollandaise sauce; Jane, the bean queen and Michael and Leslie with whom I love to cook. Thanks to my editors, Catsou Roberts (soeur), Robin Langley Sommer and Sara Hunt who made even my writing sing. Thanks to M. F. K. Fisher who inspired this book and finally, thanks to the Italians who brought me artichokes.

The publisher would like to thank the following individuals for their advice, expertise, and assistance in the preparation of this book: Julia Banks Rubel, Christopher Berlingo, Wendy Ciaccia, Nicola J. Gillies, Emily Elizabeth Head and Catherine Sylvia Reiss Antique Prints.

Thanks also to the following individuals and institutions who supplied photographs and illustrations for the following pages: **AKG, London:** 2; **Author's Collection:** 13t, 14, 17b, 42, 52, 60t, 63, 76b, 80, 95; **Avocado Commission:** 70b, 71; **British Film Institute, Department of Still Photographs:** 78t; **California Artichoke Advisory Board:** 72; **California Table Grape Commission:** 36b; **Corbis-Bettmann:** 27t, 28, 35, 41t, 48, 52b, 61, 82, 92, 93; **CorelDraw:** 11, 31b, 77; **Digital Vision Ltd.:** 30b, 60b, 75, 78b, 88, 90t; **EarthStar Stock, Inc.:** 17t, 19t, 34t, 57t, 58b, 62, 70t, 94; **Fine Art Photographic Library Ltd.:** 4, 8, 12, 32, 37, 39, 50, 63t, 74; **H.J. Heinz & Co:** 57b, 91; **Mary Evans Picture Library:** 18t, 21, 22, 25b, 27b, 40t, 41b, 47, 54, 65, 86, 90b; **Mushroom Council:** 81; **North West Cherry Growers:** 15; **Planet Art:** 10b, 19b, 24, 25t, 36t, 44t, 45b, 46, 55, 58t, 68, 76t, 85; **Saraband Image Library:** 20t, 23, 38, 45t, 69, 83, 84; © **Michael A. Smith Photography:** 43; © **Charles J. Ziga:** 13b, 26, 29, 33, 34b, 44b, 49, 87. The illustrations on pp 10t, 16, 20b, 56, 64, 66, 73 and 89 are copyright © 1998 by **Donna Ruff**.

# BIBLIOGRAPHY

### Primary Sources

Bianchini, F. and Corbetta, F. *The Complete Book of Fruits & Vegetables*. New York: Crown Publishers, Inc. 1973.

Friedlander, Barbara. *Vegetables, Fruits and Nuts*. New York: Gosset & Dunlap. 1974

Grigson, Jane. *Jane Grigson's Fruit Book*. New York: Atheneum. 1982.

Grigson, Jane. *Jane Grigson's Vegetable Book*. England: Penguin Books Ltd. 1979.

Lang, Jenifer Harvey, Ed. *Laroussse Gastronomique*. New York: Crown Publishers, Inc. 1988.

Murdich, Jack. *Buying Produce*. New York: Hearst Books. 1986.

Skinner, Charles M. *Myths and Legends of Trees, Fruits and Plants*. Philadelphia: J.B. Lippincott Co. 1911

Root, Waverly. *Food, An Authoritative and Visual History and Dictionary of the Foods of the World*. New York: Simon and Schuster. 1980.

### Secondary Sources

Payne, R.R. and Speyer Senior, D. *Cooking with Fruit*. New York: Crown Publishers. 1992.

Riely, Elizabeth. *A Feast of Fruits*. New York: Macmillian Publishing. 1993.

Chalmers, Irena. *The Great Food Almanac*. San Franscisco: Collins Publishers. 1994.

Tannahill, Reay. *Food in History*. New York: Stein and Day. 1973